W9-AAF-337

Areas in the USSR from which
the stories in this collection
have been taken

S. R.

TATARS

TATARS

ALTAY

TOFALARS

Lake Baikal

BURYATIA

TUVA

MONGOLIAN REPUBLIC

HINA

THE KAHA BIRD

Tales from the Steppes of Central Asia

THE KAHA BIRD

TALES FROM THE STEPPES OF CENTRAL ASIA

TRANSLATED AND EDITED

BY MIRRA GINSBURG

DRAWINGS BY RICHARD CUFFARI

CROWN PUBLISHERS, INC.

NEW YORK

TABLE OF CONTENTS

INTRODUCTION

THIS is the second in a series of collections of non-Russian folk tales from Russia. The first, *The Master of the Winds*, drew upon the tales of northern Siberia. The stories in this book come from the southern part of Siberia and the region southeast of the Urals known as Central Asia. The land in these regions varies greatly: wooded mountains, lakes, rivers, vast stretches of grassland known as the steppe, and arid, sandy deserts. The winters are usually very cold, and the summers very hot. Most of the peoples living here have been livestock breeders from times immemorial, with hunting and agriculture taking second place. They have been nomads, wandering in small family groups, taking their sheep, horses, goats, and camels from pasture to pasture, living in tents of various shapes, and facing the rigors of their existence with strength and a great deal of humor.

But not all life in these regions has been rural. There are also great cities of legendary fame—Bokhara, Samarkand, Khiva, and others—ancient centers of commerce between East and West. Caravans loaded with rich wares plied the deserts and steppes, establishing contact between distant lands and bringing about an exchange of cultural influences. Another source of cultural interchange were religious pilgrims, Moslem and Christian, and rare European travelers like Marco Polo. In the thirteenth century, when the Venetian, Marco Polo, traveled east, later to describe its wonders, two Christian Uygur monks—one, by an odd coincidence, called Marcos, the other, Sauma—made the long journey west "to bow to the holy relics of Jesus Christ." Marcos was appointed the Catholicos (religious head) of all Oriental Christians and served as patriarch in Baghdad. Sauma, an ambassador of the patriarch and of Khan Argun, visited the emperor of Byzantium, Andronicus II; the king of Naples, Charles II; the French king, Philip IV, the Handsome; and the king of England.

Many of the peoples in the region are of ancient origin. They possessed advanced cultures already in the distant past. Some of these cultures were retarded, others were destroyed by the successive migrations and invasions that swept the land: the Mongol conquerors of Genghis Khan in the twelfth and early thirteenth centuries, the Mongol-Tatar Golden Horde in the thirteenth, Tamerlane in the fourteenth. Yet in a sense they also served as unifying factors, carrying some of the achievements of the more advanced peoples to the more backward ones. These various conquerors established vast states that lasted for some time, then fell apart, many of the invaders drawing back, others remaining and forming small princedoms—khanates—or merging with the local population. Thus, most of the peoples in the area are of mixed origin, usually speaking various forms of Turkic dialects. The majority of them are Moslems, although some (particularly those of southern Siberia, like the Tuvans and many Buryats) are Buddhists, influenced by the proximity of Mongolia, China, and India. There are also many Christians among the Buryats.

Buryatia was annexed by Russia in the seventeenth century; the Tuvan and Altayan areas in the eighteenth; but the extensive Central Asian lands became a part of Russia only in the nineteenth century.

Chinese, Persian, and especially Indian influences are felt in the folklore of the region. Many versions of the same tales are found in the literatures of the various peoples, yet each is usually shaped by the local conditions and character and becomes unique in itself. There are also many lovely variations on European folk tales.

The most important categories of tales told by the peoples of this region are ancient heroic epics dating back to the wars of the distant past, tales of magical adventures and transformations, tales about animals, and tales from everyday life. Dragons, monsters, giants, witches, and peris (heavenly maidens, somewhat equivalent to the Western fairies) abound in the magical tales. Most of these are hostile to man, but some are friendly and helpful. There is often a close relationship between man and animals, in which the man understands animal language, or animals speak in human language. In many tales supernatural beings, birds, or animals marry humans and produce children who become mighty heroes. There is a large number of short animal tales in the form of satirical fables. But most of the humor typical of the area is concentrated in the tales from daily life. There is great delight in wisdom, wit, and cunning, especially when it is used to get the best of the powerful—the tyrannical khan, the sultan, the bey, or the large landowner whose taxes, injustice, and oppression were heavy burdens to the poor. Wit is admired as greatly as courage and strength. Skillful liars, ragged tricksters like Aldar Kose, wise men like Mirali and Hodja Nasreddin, are folk heroes as widely beloved as the mighty warriors who conquered frightful monsters and saved people and cities from destruction.

I have tried in this book to include some of the most characteristic tales of the region. Many of these have been collected only in recent years by scholars seeking to preserve the priceless heritage of folk culture before it disappears under the pressures of the industrial development that is already transforming much of the land and its peoples. Yet there are still men and women who remember the stories they heard from their parents and grandparents as well as from wandering tellers of tales, and an intensive effort is being made today to record these tales for future generations.

Many of these stories are new to Russian readers, and most will undoubtedly be new to the English-speaking reader.

The following collections will continue our journey through the folk literatures of the many non-Russian peoples who have been a part of Russia for centuries but who have nevertheless preserved even to this day their own individuality and culture.

THE GOLDEN BOWL

A Buryat Tale

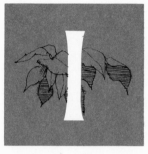n olden times there lived a khan whose name was Sanad.

One day Sanad decided to move with all his people to new lands, where pastures were richer and more abundant and life was easier. But the way to those lands was long and difficult. And so, just before the departure, Sanad issued an edict that all the old men must be killed.

"The old will be a hindrance to us on the journey. We must not take a single old man with us. Not one is to be left alive. Whoever disobeys my edict will be severely punished!"

The people were deeply grieved, but everybody feared the khan, and no one dared to disobey his cruel order.

Only one of the khan's subjects, the young Zyren, did not kill his father.

He and his father agreed that the old man would hide in a large leather sack and his son would bring him to the new lands in secret from the khan and from the others. And when they got there, they would see what could be done next.

Khan Sanad set out with all his people and all his herds from south to north, toward the distant lands. And with them, in a large leather sack laid across a horse's back, went Zyren's old father.

Secretly Zyren brought his father food and water, and late at night, when everybody was asleep, Zyren untied the sack and let the old man out to rest and stretch his numb and aching arms and legs.

They traveled for a long time, and came to a rocky seacoast. The khan ordered his followers to halt there for the night.

One of the khan's attendants went over to the edge of the rocks and noticed something gleaming deep down in the water. He looked again and saw that it was a large golden bowl of a strange, beautiful shape. He hastened immediately to the khan and told him about the precious golden bowl in the sea.

Khan Sanad cried at once that someone must dive down into the sea and bring him the bowl. But no one volunteered to do it.

Then the khan said that the men must draw lots to decide who was to go. The lot fell to one of the khan's servants. He dived in, but he never returned.

Another man was sent. He leaped down from the high, precipitous shore and also remained forever in the depths.

And so, one after another, many of the khan's men lost their lives. But the ruthless khan never dreamed of abandoning his idea. And his obedient subjects went on diving to their death.

At last, the lot was drawn by the young Zyren.

He went to the place where his father was hidden to bid the old man good bye.

"Father," said Zyren, "farewell! We shall both perish —you and I!"

"What happened?" asked the old man. "Why must you perish?"

Zyren told his father that it was his turn to dive into the sea for the bowl. "And no one has returned from there," he ended his story. "Now I will die in the sea at the khan's command, and his servants will find you and kill you . . ."

The old man listened to him and said:

"Ah, foolish people! In this way all of you will perish in the depths without ever getting the golden bowl. Don't you know that the bowl is not at the sea bottom at all? Look up at the mountain rising high over the water! The golden bowl stands at its top. What you have mistaken for the bowl is merely its reflection. How is it that none of you discovered this before?"

"What shall I do?" asked Zyren.

"Climb up the mountain, get the bowl, and bring it to the khan. It is not difficult to find, you will see it glittering from afar. But the bowl may be standing on a cliff that is too steep to climb. In that case, wait for some roe deer to appear on the mountain top, then frighten them. They will leap away and push the bowl over the edge of the cliff. Lose no time then, catch it before it drops into a deep, dark gorge!"

Zyren immediately set out toward the mountain.

It was not easy to climb to the top. He caught at bushes and trees, at sharp ledges of rock, he scraped his face and hands until they bled, he tore his clothing. At last he was almost at the very top and caught sight of the lovely golden bowl glittering at the summit of a steep, forbidding crag.

Zyren saw that he could never scale that crag. Then, as his father had advised, he began to wait for the roe deer.

He did not have to wait long. Several roes appeared atop the crag. They stood there, unafraid, looking down. Zyren shouted with all his might. The startled roe deer leaped here and there on the crag and pushed the bowl over the edge. It rolled down the side of the rock and Zyren nimbly caught it.

Joyful and pleased, with the bowl in his hands, he climbed down the mountain, came to Khan Sanad, and placed the bowl before him. The khan asked:

"How did you get the golden bowl from the sea bottom?"

"I did not get it from the sea bottom," said Zyren. "I brought it from that mountain top. In the sea there was only a reflection of it."

"But who told you about it?"

"I guessed it myself."

The khan asked no further questions and dismissed him.

On the following day Khan Sanad and all his people moved on.

After a long march, they came to a wide desert. The sun had scorched the ground and burnt all the grass. There was neither a river nor a brook as far as the eye could see, and the people began to suffer thirst. The khan sent out riders in all directions to look for water, but no one found any. There was nothing but dry, fiery earth all around. The people thought they would surely perish in the desert. No one knew what to do or where to go.

Then Zyren secretly made his way to his father and asked him:

"Father, tell me what to do! Both people and cattle are dying without water!"

The old man said:

"Release a three-year-old cow and follow her. Where she stops and sniffs the ground, there you will dig."

Zyren ran to the herds and released a three-year-old cow. The cow lowered her head and began to wander from place to place. At last she stopped and noisily began to sniff the hot earth.

"Dig here," said Zyren.

The men began to dig and soon found a large subterranean stream. A jet of cold, pure water spurted out and flowed on the ground. Everybody had enough to drink. Everybody's spirits rose.

Khan Sanad called Zyren and asked him:

"How did you find the subterranean stream in this arid place?"

"By signs," said Zyren.

The people drank their fill, rested, and went on.

They journeyed many days. Then they made camp to rest a while. At night there was an unexpected downpour which put out their fire. No matter how hard they tried, they could not start it again. Shivering, wet, they did not know what to do.

At last someone noticed a glimmering fire on a distant mountain top, and Khan Sanad sent men to bring some fire.

The men rushed to fulfill the khan's command. One, then another, then a third went up the mountain and found the fire under the dense fir tree, and the hunter who was warming himself by it. Each took a burning log to bring back to the camp, but each time the fire went out in the rain on the way back.

Khan Sanad flew into a rage and ordered that all the messengers who had been sent to fetch the fire and had returned without it be put to death.

Then it was Zyren's turn to go. He made his way to his father's hiding place and asked:

"What shall I do? How can the fire be brought safely from the mountain to the camp?"

The old man said:

"Don't take any burning logs. They will either go out on the way, or burn down, or be quenched by the rain. Take a large pot with you, fill it with live coals, and you will bring fire to the camp!"

Zyren did as his father had taught him. He brought back a potful of glowing coals. People made fires, dried themselves, cooked their food.

When the khan learned who had brought the fire, he summoned Zyren, and angrily began to scold him:

"You've known all this while how to bring the fire, yet you were silent! Why did you not say at once how it could be done?"

"I did not know it before," said Zyren.

"Then how did you learn afterward?" the khan persisted.

And he continued to question him till Zyren finally confessed that he had been able to fulfill all of the khan's commands thanks to his old father's advice.

"Where is your father?" asked the khan.

And Zyren answered:

"I've brought him all this way in a large leather sack."

Then the khan commanded that the old man be brought into his presence.

"I revoke my edict," he said. "The old are not a hindrance to the young. Old age is the age of wisdom. You need not hide any longer, you will travel openly with all the rest!"

LIVING WATER

A Tofalar Tale

his happened a long, long time ago, when the cedar, the fir, and the pine still had needles that yellowed and dropped in the fall instead of staying green all winter.

Once in those olden times a Tofalar went out into the woods to hunt. He walked and walked, and he came farther than any hunter had ever dared to go. He saw a bog so vast that no beast could have crossed it, no bird could have flown across.

And the Tofalar said to himself:

"If our animals can't run across this bog, and our birds cannot fly across it, what kinds of animals and birds live on the other side?"

The more he thought about it, the more curious he became.

"I must find out," he said to himself. "Whatever happens, I must get there."

And so he took a good running start, and leaped right clear across the bog.

He looked around: the same earth, the same grass, the same trees.

"Silly!" he said. "There was no need to jump."

Suddenly his mouth dropped open with wonder.

In a little clearing stood seven harnessed rabbits. They stood quietly, waiting. Then seven people came out of seven burrows in the earth, exactly like all people, only tiny. When the rabbits flattened their ears, the people were taller than the rabbits. When the rabbits' ears stood up, the people were smaller than the rabbits.

"Who are you?" asked the Tofalar.

"We are immortal people," said the tiny men. "We wash ourselves in living water, and we never die. And who are you?"

"I am a hunter."

The little men clapped their hands with joy.

"Oh, good! Oh, good!" they cried in chorus.

And one of them, the eldest, with white hair and a long white beard, came forward and said:

"A terrible, huge beast has come into our land. We don't know where it came from. The other day it caught one of our people and killed him. We are immortal, we never die ourselves, but this beast killed one of us. You are a hunter—can you help us in this trouble? Can you hunt down the beast?"

"Why not?" answered the Tofalar, but to himself he wondered: "Will I be able to kill such a frightful beast?"

However, he went out to track the beast. He looked and he looked, but could find nothing except rabbits' footprints. Suddenly, among the rabbit prints he noticed the track of a sable.

"Oh, that's too fine a quarry to miss," he said. "First I will get the sable, and then I'll go on looking for the terrible, huge beast."

He found the sable and killed it. Then he skinned it and went on with his search. He walked the length and breadth of the little people's land, but could not find any trace of the beast.

So he came back to the little people and said to them:

"I could not find your terrible, huge beast. All I have found was this sable." And he showed them the little sable skin.

"That's it, that's it!" they cried. "Oo-h, what a huge skin, what thick paws, what terrible, sharp claws!" And the eldest of the little men said to the Tofalar:

"You have saved us and our people! And we shall pay for your kindness with kindness. Wait for us. We'll come to visit you and bring you living water. You'll wash in it and will become immortal too."

The Tofalar jumped back across the bog and went back to his valley and told his people about the little men.

And the Tofalars began to wait for their guests, the immortal little men.

They waited one day, two days, three days, many, many days. But the guests did not come, and the Tofalars forgot about them and their promise.

Winter came. Everything around was frozen. And the bog was covered with a coat of ice.

One day the village women went to the woods to gather firewood. Suddenly they saw a little herd of rabbits galloping their way. They looked again, and saw that every rabbit was saddled, and in every saddle sat a tiny man with a little pitcher in his hands. The women burst out laughing at the sight.

"Look, look!" they cried to one another.

"They are riding on rabbits!"

"And look at the little men, how funny!"

"Oh, what a joke!"

"Oh, I'll die laughing!"

Now, the immortal people were a proud race. They took offense at this reception. The one in front, with white hair and a long beard, shouted something to the others, and all of them spilled out the contents of their pitchers onto the ground. Then the rabbits turned and hopped away so fast that you could only see their white tails flicker.

And so the Tofalars never got the living water. It went instead to the pine, the cedar, and the fir. And this is why they are fresh and green all through the year. Their needles never die.

OSKUS-OOL AND HIS
NINE RED HORSES

A Tuvan Tale

t the mouth of the seven rivers there lived an orphan named Oskus-Ool. From early childhood he worked for other people. When he got older, he went to work as a herder for Karaty-Khan. For many days and nights he led the khan's horses from pasture to pasture. One day he saw a spotted, short-tailed, earless mare in the wide steppe. He caught her and brought her to the khan.

"Is this a joke?" the khan shouted at him. "What would I want with such a mongrel beast—she doesn't even look like a horse. Let her go. Or, better still, keep her as payment of a year's wages."

Oskus-Ool took his mare and sent her out to pasture with the khan's herds. He combed her and he brushed her and looked after her. And in a year she brought him nine red colts, which soon grew into tall, strong, handsome horses.

When the khan's servants came to inspect the herd, they found the horses healthy and well fed, with many new colts. But the best and handsomest of all the horses were the nine red stallions that followed the spotted mare.

The servants came back to the khan and told him:

"The herds are doing well, the horses are well fed and healthy, and there is a great increase in the herd. But the finest and most thoroughbred of all are the nine red stallions led by Oskus-Ool's short-tailed spotted mare. They put the rest of all your heards to shame."

"We must kill Oskus-Ool," said the khan, "and take his nine red horses. Ride out and tell him I want to see him tonight."

When Oskus-Ool heard the khan's summons, he galloped at full speed to Karaty's tent. On the way he met an old man who was herding calves. The old man said to Oskus-Ool:

"We are both poor men, and I want to help you. The khan means to kill you tonight and seize your nine red horses. Don't spend the night in the khan's tent."

"Thanks, grandfather," said Oskus-Ool.

He came to the khan's camp, entered his tent, and bowed.

"The horses you are herding are well cared for, and there is a goodly increase in the herd," Karaty-Khan said to him. "You've worked hard and you have earned a rest.

Spend the night in my yurt. Eat, drink, and have a good night's sleep." The khan spoke kindly, hiding his black thoughts.

Oskus-Ool ate and drank, and then he said:

"I thank you, khan. But the herd led by the roan stallion has wandered off too far. It's on the other side of the Arzaita hills. I'll bring it back and leave it with your servants, then I'll come back and rest."

Oskus-Ool ran out of the yurt, leaped on his horse, and sped toward the herd. He gathered his nine red horses, mounted one of them, and said to the short-tailed spotted mare:

"Go free, eat grass, drink water." Then he galloped south.

He slept that night in the wide open steppe. In the morning he found that one red horse had been devoured by a wolf.

"Well," he said sadly," what can I do? I still have eight fine horses."

He moved away with his horses to the mouth of the six rivers. But that night the wolf came again and ate another horse.

He moved to the mouth of the five rivers, thinking: The wolf won't find us here. But that night another horse was gone.

And so he wandered from place to place, and every night the wolf devoured another of his horses until there was only one left.

I am a poor man again, he thought. I have a single horse, and I won't let the wolf get this one. He galloped farther south, away from the rivers.

When night came, he bound the horse to his hand by a long rope, and tried to stay awake. But after a while his head fell down on his chest, and he was fast asleep. In the morning he woke and saw the wolf greedily finishing what was left of his last horse.

Oskus-Ool seized his bow and his arrow with the iron tip, and pulled the bowstring, ready to release the arrow.

"Don't kill me!" the wolf cried in a human voice. "I am Beriu, son of the khan of all the wolves. I'm coming back from war in the northern lands. My army perished, and I alone survived. Your horses kept me alive on the long journey home. My village is not far, just over that yellow mountain. Go to the white yurt, where my father lives. I'll tell him what has happened, and he will offer you all manner of wealth. You will be paid well for the loss of your horses."

"There's nothing to be done now," sighed Oskus-Ool, and made Beriu swear to keep his promise.

He slung the saddle over his shoulder and went to the yellow mountain. On the way he met an old man who was herding lambs.

"Peace to you, grandfather," Oskus-Ool greeted him respectfully.

"Who are you?" asked the old man. "Where is your

encampment, and where are you going, my son?"

"My name is Oskus-Ool. I was the horseherd of Ka-raty-Khan, who is a greedy and a cruel man. He wanted to take away my nine red horses and to kill me. I ran away and took my horses with me. But Beriu, son of the khan of all the wolves, devoured them one by one. Instead, he promised that his father will give me cattle from his herds and goods from his goods. And now I am going there."

"Listen to my advice, my son. Refuse whatever he offers you. Say only: 'I will accept three grains of gold, three poles from your yurt, the little yellow dog at your feet, and the small iron box in the corner.'"

Oskus-Ool entered the large white yurt and saw a huge gray wolf sitting on a silver dais. Oskus-Ool bowed to him and said:

"Good health to you, venerable khan! I hope you and your herds are doing well."

"And how is your health?" asked the old wolf. "And are your herds doing well?"

"My own health is fine," replied Oskus-Ool, "but I have no herds. I had nine red horses, but your son devoured them all. I've come to you with a complaint. What will you pay me for my loss?"

The old wolf said:

"Would you like a herd of my own horses?"

"No," said Oskus-Ool. "I don't need your horses. Your son will come again and kill them."

"Then take a herd of camels."

But Oskus-Ool refused the camels.

"If you want no camels, take bulls and cows—as many as you wish."

But Oskus-Ool refused the bulls and cows, and he refused a flock of sheep.

"What do you want, then, my friend?" asked the old wolf.

"Your little yellow dog, three poles from your yurt, three grains of gold, and that small iron box in the corner."

"And what will you do with them?" asked the wolf.

"I'll stick the poles into the ground, tie their tops, and I will have a yurt to sleep in. The little yellow dog will follow me everywhere. As for the three grains of gold and the iron box, I'll find good use for them."

The old wolf gave him what he asked. Then he looked at the presents and laughed. He looked at them again and wept.

And Oskus-Ool returned with his presents to the field where the old man was grazing his lambs.

"Why did I listen to you, old man? I hoped to get all sorts of goods for my red horses, and I came away with nothing worth while," cried Oskus-Ool in anger.

"Don't say that, my son. You will have good use of these presents. When you come to a place where there are rocks and woods, water and grass, throw the three grains of gold in three different directions. Then stick the poles in the ground and tie their tops. Pat the little yellow dog on the head, put the iron box beside you, and go to sleep. In the morning you will see that I advised you well."

"We'll see," said Oskus-Ool, and started on his way.

He walked and walked until he came to Kara-Khem, a place where there were rocks and woods, water and grass. He threw the three gold grains in different directions, set up his yurt, patted the little yellow dog on the head, put the iron box beside him, and went to sleep.

In the morning Oskus-Ool awakened, looked around, and did not believe his eyes. He was lying in a white yurt, so large that ninety horses could not surround it. Along the walls of the yurt stood trunks of gold and silver. The floor was covered with soft, rich felt. In the middle of the yurt a fire was blazing in the fireplace, and a young woman, so beautiful that she spread the radiance of the sun and moon around her, was making tea.

What happened? Oskus-Ool asked himself. Is this a dream, or is it real?

"Who are you?" he asked the maiden.

"I am the Golden Princess, your wife," she said.

"And whose yurt is this?"

"Ours. Get up, we shall have tea!"

She picked up his old, ragged robe lying near the door and threw it to Oskus-Ool. A new silk robe fell at his feet. She threw to him his old, worn boots, and new embroidered ones fell at his feet. He dressed, went out of the yurt and looked around: herds of horses, camels, cows, and sheep were grazing as far as the eye could see.

"Where has all this come from?" asked Oskus-Ool.

"You got fine presents from the old wolf," the princess laughed. "He is a great wizard. I was bewitched and turned into that little yellow dog, but your request restored me to my human self."

She poured tea from a silver teapot into two silver cups. They drank and laughed with joy. And so they lived together—young, handsome, happy, lacking nothing, rich in clothing and horses and camels and cows and sheep.

One day the Golden Princess took two silver pitchers and went down to the river for water. At that moment, Karaty-Khan's vizier was riding by. He halted for a moment, stared at the Golden Princess, and rode off full speed to the khan. He told the khan about Oskus-Ool's great wealth and beautiful young wife. And the khan sent off a messenger to summon Oskus-Ool.

"Let's play a game of hide and seek," Karaty-Khan said to Oskus-Ool. "Each of us will hide three times. If you find me, you can have my wife. If I find you, I'll take yours."

And Oskus-Ool went sadly back to the Golden Princess.

"What happened?" she asked him.

"The khan has ordered me to play a game of hide and

seek with him. Each of us must hide three times. Who- ever finds the other will take his wife. If they take you away, I'll surely die. I cannot live without you. To- morrow the khan will hide, and I must find him."

"And where do you mean to look for him?" asked the Golden Princess.

"Everywhere: in the yard, in the steppe, in the yurt, under the trunks, in the bed."

"No, you will not find him there. In the khan's camp there are three yurts. Go into the middle one. You will see the khan's wife and, on the trunk behind her, three black sable hats. Ask her to sell you one. Then take the middle one and try to tear off the ribbon sewn on it."

The next day Oskus-Ool did as his wife advised him. He entered the white yurt, picked up the middle hat, and said to the khan's wife:

"This is a handsome hat! Perhaps you'll sell it to me?" and he began to tear away the ribbon.

"Ouch! Stop it! You're tearing off my ears!" the hat cried and turned into Karaty-Khan.

That night the Golden Princess said to her husband:

"Don't worry, go to sleep. I'll help you hide tomorrow so that the khan will never find you."

On the next day the khan brought his whole army to the tent of Oskus-Ool. They looked at every tree and every stone around the yurt, but could not find him.

Then the khan came into the yurt and turned speech- less at the sight of the Golden Princess. She was sitting by the fire and sewing.

"Can't you speak?" she asked.

And finally he answered:

"I could not find your Oskus-Ool anywhere."

"You truly could not find him?" she asked, and threw the needle on the floor. Before him stood Oskus-Ool, laughing.

The next day it was the khan's turn to hide.

"Where do you mean to look for him?" the Golden Princess asked Oskus-Ool.

"I will tear all his hats, and one of them will probably cry 'Stop!' and turn into the khan."

"You will not find him this way," said the princess. "Behind the khan's yurt, before the steep dark cliff, there are three willow shrubs. Pull out the middle one and start carving it with your knife, saying: 'This willow branch will make a handsome handle for my whip.'"

Early at dawn Oskus-Ool came to the steep black cliff, pulled out the middle willow shrub, and began to carve it, repeating:

"I'll make a handsome handle for my whip."

"Ouch, stop it! You almost cut my nose off, Oskus-Ool!" cried the willow and turned into Karaty-Khan.

And now it was the turn of Oskus-Ool again. Once more the khan and all his army turned every stone and counted every tree. They looked among the herds and all around the yurt.

"Where are you, Oskus-Ool?" cried the khan?

Then he entered the yurt:

"I could not find your Oskus-Ool."

"You truly could not find him?" asked the princess. Then she took off her ring and threw it toward the khan. And he saw Oskus-Ool standing before him, laughing.

The next day was the khan's turn.

"Where do you mean to look for him?" the Golden Princess asked Oskus-Ool.

"I'll cut down all the willow shrubs before the steep black cliff, and I will tear the ribbons off all the hats."

"No, you will not find him this way. Tomorrow morning a herd of cows will come out to pasture from the khan's camp. Among them you will see a bluish-white one-horned bull. Seize him by the horn and twist his head with all your strength."

And Oskus-Ool did as his wife advised him. When he seized the bull by his single horn and began to twist his head, the bull began to bellow:

"Ouch, stop, stop! You almost tore my head off!" and the khan stood red with anger before Oskus-Ool.

Now it was Oskus-Ool's last turn to hide.

On the next morning the khan again brought his whole army with him. They counted every tree and every stone, they looked all over the woods and the meadows. Then the khan with seven of his warriors came into the yurt and looked through all the clothing, all the rugs, but Oskus-Ool was nowhere to be found.

And in the meantime the Golden Princess sat and combed her lovely hair with a fine silver comb.

"Come out, come out, Oskus-Ool, I cannot find you," cried the khan.

"Why should he come out?" asked the princess. "He has been here before you all the time."

She threw down her comb, and Oskus-Ool stood before the khan, laughing.

"Well," he said. "I've won three times, but I don't need your wife. All I want is to be left alone to live in peace with my Golden Princess."

But Karaty-Khan was cruel and greedy. He refused to accept defeat. The next day he summoned Oskus-Ool again and said to him:

"It's true that you defeated me in the game of hide and seek. But this is not the end. I want you to go to the woods and count the number of rabbits living there. If you don't, I'll take away your wife."

Oskus-Ool returned to his yurt, his face dark with sorrow.

"What happened now?" asked his wife. "What new disaster has befallen?"

"Karaty-Khan wants me to count how many rabbits live in the woods and mountains, or he will come and take you from me. How can I do it?"

"That's simple," said the Golden Princess. "Go to sleep, and in the morning you will go into the woods."

In the morning she mixed a tasty dish of flour and salt in a wooden bowl, woke Oskus-Ool, and said to him:

"Go out into the woods, put this bowl under a tree, and hide, but listen well."

After a little time a large rabbit came running by. He started eating the flour and salt, and when he finished he said:

"There are eighty thousand rabbits in the woods, and sixty thousand in the mountains, but none of them has ever had such a tasty meal!"

The rabbit hopped away, and Oskus-Ool came to Karaty-Khan and said to him:

"There are eighty thousand rabbits in the woods, and sixty thousand in the mountains. If you don't believe me, go and count them yourself."

Karaty-Khan looked at him, then he said:

"You answered that. Now go to the highest mountain, to the cave of the old gray bear, the grandfather of all the bears. Find out how old he is. If you don't, you'll lose your wife."

Again Oskus-Ool went sadly home to his wife and told her of Karaty's new demand.

"Lie down to sleep now. Tomorrow you will climb the mountain."

Oskus-Ool fell asleep, and the Golden Princess went to work. She made forty tiny dolls, dressed them all in fur hats and silken robes, and put them into a sieve. In the morning she awakened Oskus-Ool and told him:

"Climb up the mountain and find the old bear's cave. Put this sieve near the entrance, hide well behind a rock, and listen."

Oskus-Ool climbed the mountain, found the old bear's cave, placed the sieve with the tiny dolls near the entrance, and hid behind a large gray rock. He sat and waited. Soon a great bear lumbered out of the cave, approached the sieve, looked at the dolls, and said:

"I've lived in this world sixty-two years, I've seen a lot of wonders in my lifetime, but I've never seen such tiny men before!"

He said it, and climbed back into his cave. And Oskus-Ool came running to Karaty-Khan:

"The old great bear is sixty-two years old. He told me so himself!"

At this, Karaty-Khan flew into a rage. His face turned green, then purple.

"If I can't get your wife by peaceful means, I will wage war on you. Tomorrow you'll be dead, and I will have the Golden Princess."

This time Oskus-Ool came to his wife and wept.

"The khan is going to wage war on us. How can I fight him? I guess this is my end, and you will not escape him, either."

But the Golden Princess smiled and said:

"It is not meet for a man to cry. But do not worry. Karaty-Khan won't reach us. Neither will he return to his own camp. Now let us go to sleep; tomorrow we shall be rid of him forever."

Oskus-Ool went to bed. At dawn he heard a noise in the distance. He went outside and saw the armies of Karaty-Khan approaching. He ran back into the yurt and cried to his wife:

"They're coming!"

"It's early," she said. "Go back to sleep."

The noise grew louder. There was a stamping of hooves and a clashing of armor. Oskus-Ool ran out and saw Karaty-Khan and his warriors still nearer.

"It's early," said his wife again. "Go back to sleep."

Before long, an arrow flew into the yurt.

"Now is just the time," said the Golden Princess. "Do you remember the little iron box the old wolf gave you? Put it outside the door and open it."

Oskus-Ool brought out the little iron box, put it outside the door, and opened the lid. A torrent of water gushed from the box, spreading wider and deeper. It swept the khan and all his armies straight into the river, and carried them far, far out to the sea. They drowned, and no one ever heard of them again.

And Oskus-Ool had no more enemies. He lived a long and happy life with his radiant and lovely Golden Princess.

TORKO-CHACHAK—
THE SILKEN TASSEL

An Altay Tale

here was a girl called Torko-Cha-chak, which means "Silken Tassel." Her eyes were like wild cherries, her brows were like two rainbows. Into her braids she plaited seashells from distant lands, and on her hat there was a silken tassel, white as moonlight.

One day the father of Silken Tassel fell ill, and her mother said to her:

"Get up on the bay horse and hurry to the bank of the rushing river. There, in a tent made of birchbark, you will find the shaman Teldekpei. Ask him to come here and to cure your father."

The girl leaped up on the bay horse with the white star on his forehead, took in her right hand the leather reins with silver rings and in her left, the lash with a finely carved bone handle.

The bay horse galloped fast, the reins shook up and down, the harness tinkled merrily.

Old Teldekpei sat at the threshold of his birchbark tent. With a sharp knife, he was carving a round cup out of a piece of birchwood. He heard the merry clattering of hooves, the ringing of the harness. He raised his eyes and saw the girl on the bay horse.

She sat proudly in the high saddle, the silken tassel fluttered in the wind, the seashells sang in her thick braids.

The knife dropped from the shaman's hand, the cup rolled into the fire.

"Grandfather," said the girl. "My father is sick, come help us."

"I will cure your father, Silken Tassel, if you will marry me."

The shaman's eyebrows were like moss, his white beard, like a thorny shrub.

Frightened, Silken Tassel pulled the reins and galloped off.

"At dawn tomorrow I will come to you!" the shaman called after her.

The girl came home, entered the tent and said:

"Old Teldekpei will be here tomorrow at dawn."

The stars had not yet melted in the sky, the people in the camp had not yet set the milk out to ferment, the meat in the kettles had not yet been cooked, and the fine white rugs were not yet spread upon the ground when

there was a loud clattering of hooves.

The oldest of the elders came out to welcome the mighty shaman Teldekpei.

He sat atop a shaggy horse with a back as wide as a mountain yak's. Silently, looking at no one, he dismounted, and, greeting no one, he went into the tent. The old men brought in after him the eighty-pound robe in which he worked his magic and put it down on the white rug. They hung his tambourine upon a wooden peg and made a fire of fragrant juniper twigs under it.

All day, from dawn to sunset, the shaman sat without lifting his eyelids, without moving, without uttering a word.

Late at night Teldekpei stood up and pulled his red shaman's hat down to his eyebrows. Two owl feathers stood up in his hat like ears; red strips of cloth fluttered behind it like two wings. Large glass beads fell upon his face like hail. Groaning, he lifted from the rug his eighty-pound robe and put his hands into the stiff, hard sleeves. Along the sides of the robe hung frogs and snakes woven of magic grasses. Feathers of woodpeckers were stuck into its back.

The Shaman took his tambourine from the peg and struck it with a wooden stick. A booming noise filled the tent, like a mountain storm in winter. The people stood about chilled with fear. The shaman danced and swayed and worked his magic, the bells rang, and the tambourine clashed and moaned and thundered. Then sudden silence fell. The tambourine moaned for the last time, and everything was still.

Teldekpei sank onto the white rug, wiped the sweat off his brow with his sleeve, straightened his tangled beard with his fingers, took the heart of a goat from a tray, ate it, and said:

"Drive out Silken Tassel. An evil spirit resides in her. While she is in the camp, her father will not get up from his illness. Misfortune will not leave this valley. Little children will fall asleep forever; their fathers and grandfathers will die in torment."

The women of the camp fell down upon the ground in fear. The old men pressed their hands over their eyes with grief. The young men looked at Silken Tassel; twice they turned red, and twice they turned pale.

"Put Silken Tassel into a wooden barrel," the shaman boomed. "Bind the barrel with nine iron hoops. Nail down the bottom with copper nails, and throw the barrel into the rushing river."

He said this, mounted his shaggy horse, and rode off to his own white tent.

"Hey!" he shouted to his slaves. "Go to the river! The water will bring down a large barrel. Catch it and bring it here, then run into the woods. If you hear weeping, do not turn back. If cries and moans spread through the woods, do not look back. Do not return to my tent in less than three days."

For seven days and seven nights the people of the

encampment could not bring themselves to carry out the shaman's orders. For seven days and seven nights they bid the girl farewell. On the eighth day they put Silken Tassel into a wooden barrel, bound it with nine iron hoops, nailed down the bottom with copper nails, and threw the barrel into the rushing river.

On that day a young fisherman called Balykchi sat on the steep bank of the river some distance from the camp.

He saw the barrel, caught it, brought it into his hut, picked up an axe, and knocked out the bottom. When he saw the girl, the hand that held the axe dropped, and his heart leaped like a grasshopper. At last he asked the girl:

"What is your name?"

"Silken Tassel—Torko-Chachak."

The girl climbed out of the barrel and bowed low to the fisherman.

"Who put you into the barrel?"

"The shaman Teldekpei said that it must be done."

The fisherman whistled for his dog, fierce as a mountain lion, put him into the barrel, nailed down the bottom with copper nails, and let the barrel float downstream.

The shaman's slaves pulled out the barrel, brought it to the white birchbark tent, put it before the old wizard, and ran away into the woods.

But even before they reached the woods, they heard

the shaman call: "Help! Help!"

But the slaves did everything he had bidden. They heard shouts, but did not turn back. They heard moaning and cries, but did not look back. For such were their master's orders.

Three days later they returned from the woods. The shaman lay on the ground, more dead than alive. His clothes were torn to shreds, his beard was bloody and tangled, his eyebrows were shaggier than ever.

And Torko-Chachak remained with the young fisherman in the green hut. But Balykchi did not go out fishing any more. He would pick up the rod and take two steps toward the river, then look back at the girl on the threshold, and his feet carried him back to her. He could not get enough of gazing at Silken Tassel.

And so the girl took a piece of birchbark and painted her face on it with the juice of flowers and berries. She nailed the birchbark to a stick and put the stick into the ground right by the water. Now the fisherman was not so lonely by the river. The painted Torko-Chachak looked at him as if she were alive.

One day Balykchi looked at the picture and did not notice when a large fish caught his bait. The rod slipped from his hand and knocked down the stick, and the birchbark fell into the water and floated away.

When the girl heard this, she wept and wailed, she rubbed her brows with her hands, she tangled her braids with her fingers.

"Whoever finds the birchbark will come here! Hurry, hurry, Balykchi, and try to catch it! Turn your goatskin coat with the fur outside, get up on the blue ox, and ride as fast as he will go along the riverbank."

Balykchi put on his goatskin coat with the fur outside. He mounted the blue ox and galloped off along the riverbank. But the painted birchbark floated down and down, faster and faster. Balykchi could not catch it.

The water brought the birchbark to the mouth of the river. Here it got tangled in a willow branch and hung over the rapid current.

At the mouth of that river, the camp of rich and cruel Kara-Khan spread far and wide over endless fields and meadows. Innumerable herds of cattle, white and red, were grazing in the tall grass.

The shepherds noticed the white birchbark in the willows. They came down nearer and stared at it, enchanted. Their hats were blown off by the wind and floated down the current. Their herds wandered away and scattered in the woods.

"What is this?" thundered Kara-Khan, riding up to his shepherds. "Hey, lazy good-for-nothings! What holiday is this? Whose wedding are you celebrating?"

He raised his nine-tailed lash, but suddenly he saw the birchbark, and the lash dropped from his hand.

A girl looked at him from the birchbark. Her lips were like a newly opened scarlet flower, her eyes were like wild cherries, her brows like two rainbows, her lashes like arrows that struck the heart.

He snatched the birchbark, put it into the bosom of his coat, and shouted in a terrifying voice:

"Hey, you! Mighty fighters, strong men, warriors, heroes! Get on your horses at once! If we don't find this girl, I'll kill you with my spear, I'll shoot you with my arrows, I'll have you thrown into boiling water!"

He touched the reins and galloped off upstream. Behind him came an army of warriors, clanking their heavy armor of red copper and yellow bronze.

Behind the army rode the stablemen leading a white stallion that was as fast as thought.

At the sight of this dread army, Silken Tassel did not cry and did not laugh. Silently she mounted the white stallion with the pearl-embroidered saddle.

And so, without crying, without laughing, without saying a word to anyone, without answering anyone, Torko-Chachak sat in the khan's tent.

Suddenly, one sunny morning, she sprang outside, clapped her hands, and laughed, and sang!

Kara-Khan looked where she was looking, ran where she was running, and saw a young man in a goatskin coat turned inside out mounted on a blue ox.

"So it was he who made you laugh, Silken Tassel? Why, I can do the same. I can also put on this ragged coat. I can also mount the blue ox without fear. Then smile as gaily to me, sing to me as merrily!"

And Kara-Khan tore the goatskin coat from Balykchi's

shoulders, went over to the blue ox, picked up the reins, and put his foot into the iron stirrup.

"Moo-oo! Moo-oo!" bellowed the ox, and, giving the khan no time to swing his right foot over the saddle, he dragged him off over the hills and valleys.

Kara-Khan's black cruel liver burst with shame. His round cruel heart burst with rage.

And Silken Tassel took the poor fisherman Balykchi by the right hand, and together they returned to their green hut.

May you, too, find the happiness they found, for this is the end of our tale.

THREE DAUGHTERS

A Tatar Tale

nce there lived a woman who had three daughters. She toiled day and night to feed and dress and bring them up. And the three daughters grew up swift as swallows and lovely as the moon.

One after the other they married and went to live with their husbands.

Several years went by. The mother grew older, and one day she got sick. From day to day she felt worse, and finally she called a brown squirrel who lived in the tree outside her window and asked her:

"Run to my daughters, little friend, and tell them I am sick and want to see them. But hurry!"

"Oh," sighed the eldest when she heard the sad news from the squirrel. "Oh, I'd be glad to come, but I must first finish polishing these two brass trays."

"These two brass trays?" the squirrel cried angrily. "Then may you be forever stuck to them!"

And the trays suddenly slipped off the table and clung to the girl, one in front, and one in back. She fell down on the floor and crawled out of the house—a large brown turtle.

Then the squirrel knocked at the middle daughter's window.

"Oh," sighed the daughter. "I'd be glad to run to see my mother this very minute, but I must finish weaving this cloth in time for market day."

"So!" cried the angry squirrel. "Now you will weave without ceasing all your life long!"

And the second daughter turned into a spider.

When the squirrel knocked at the youngest daughter's window, she was mixing dough. Without a word, without even stopping to wipe her hands, the girl ran to her mother.

"May you always bring joy to people, my dear child," said the squirrel. "And everyone will love and cherish you, and your children, and your children's children."

And the third daughter lived many, many years, and everybody loved her. And when she died, she turned into a golden bee.

All summer, day in, day out, the bee is gathering honey for people, and its front paws are always yellow with sweet dough. But in winter, when everything around dies and freezes with the cold, the bee sleeps in its warm hive, and when it wakes, it eats sugar and honey.

THREE MAIDENS

A Kazakh Tale

t is said there was a time, long, long ago, when seven suns rose every day over our mountains. The suns' rays, like milk, fed everything that lived. Grasses and trees grew taller and stronger every year. And the people who lived at the foot of the mountains grew happier and richer and more beautiful from generation to generation. For seven suns shone over the country. Our peasants reaped seven harvests every year, and the piles of grain rose higher than the mountain peaks. For seven suns shone over our country. Animals bore their young seven times every year; cows and sheep wandered over the mountains and meadows, and they were more numerous than the green branches on the pine trees growing on the mountains. For seven suns shone over our country.

The music of shepherd pipes was carried everywhere by the light breeze. The fields resounded with constant laughter and songs. People sang praises to the god of the suns and to time, which was as sweet as honey.

When the clouds of evening floated over the mountain range and the last sunrays disappeared, the Kazakh peasants and cattle breeders gathered around old trees, in the fields, and on the river banks to sing the evening prayer:

Allah! Allah!
Protect! Preserve!
Let the seven suns in the sky
Sink calmly to rest,
And rise again to greet us in the morning!
Allah! Allah!
Protect! Preserve!

Years passed, and the seven suns continued to brighten the sky, and the Kazakhs lived happy lives.

But one day an evil spirit, a shaitan, appeared in an old mountain canyon. He saw the joy of all who lived around him in the country, and he swore:

"I shall not rest until I knock all seven suns out of the sky!"

The shaitan was the son of a hundred-year-old owl, and from his very birth he loved darkness and was afraid of light. He began to think of how to kill the suns and bring eternal darkness to the earth. And he devised a cunning plan.

By magic, he turned himself into a hundred winged

men with eagle beaks. They spread their wings and flew to the highest mountain top. And every day they sent their steel arrows at the suns.

They shot down one sun, then another, then the third, the fourth, the fifth, the sixth . . .

The Kazakhs stood by helplessly, watching the disappearance of their suns. All day they prayed and wept, but there was nothing they could do.

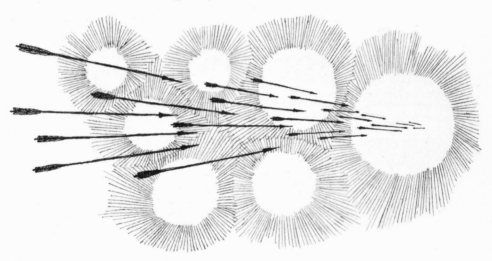

And then the last, the seventh sun was shot down by a keen steel arrow. Eternal darkness descended on the mountains. In the valleys the trees and grasses lost the sap of life. The grain dried out in the fields. The cows and sheep died in the mountains and meadows. The illimitable orchards turned into dead wood, suitable only for making fires. Death-dealing clouds hung low over the Kazahks. They faced famine and cold. They prayed, but hope went out of their hearts.

Then one day three brave maidens came before the people. They bowed first to the old men, then to the rest, and proudly said to them:

"Grandfathers, mothers, brothers, and sisters! Permit us to go forth to seek the suns and bring them back. We shall either find them, or perish in strange lands. Farewell!"

And the three maidens set out on their perilous journey. They felt their way in darkness. No one knows how many steep mountains they climbed, how many high ridges they crossed, how many wide rivers they swam across and how many narrow streams they forded. And who knows how much they suffered from parching heat and bitter cold! Their garments tore and hung in shreds; their feet were sore and weary, their hair had grown so long that it trailed after them upon the ground like mountain mist. But while their hearts were beating they steadfastly went on and on. Where were the suns? They did not know. Would they ever succeed in finding them? They did not know. But, never despairing, they went ever forward, step after step.

And one day there was thunder in the sky, and lightning flashed around them. In the blaze they saw an old, old man with long white hair. His eyes gleamed with a golden light, and he spoke gently to the maidens:

"Brave maidens, your resolution is stronger than the mountain peaks! Your hearts are purer than the snow on the highest mountains! You need no longer wander in search of the lost suns—stand here and wait! A fiery rider will gallop past you on a chestnut horse with flaming mane and tail, and every time you see him one of the suns will come back to the skies. It will take many ages before all seven return to the Kazakh steppes, but if your patience equals your courage, they will come! Remember my words!"

The thunder ceased. The lightning vanished. The old man was gone. And all that could be heard now in the silence was the triumphant laughter of the three brave maidens.

In the morning, the fiery rider galloped past them on the chestnut horse with flaming mane and tail, and after him the sun rose bright and gay and lighted up the mountains and meadows. The Kazakhs praised Allah and went back to tending their fields and orchards, their cows and sheep. But they never forgot the three brave maidens.

Many years and many centuries have gone. The maidens kept their promise to the people. They died a long, long time ago, but on the spot where they had stood, amid the endless steppe, three mighty peaks rise high into the sky. Every morning, they are the first to see the sun, and they will wait, as they have promised, for the fiery rider to gallop past again and again, until all seven suns are back over our land. The mountains are called the Three Maidens.

TWO TRICKSTERS

A Kazakh Tale

ong ago, when donkeys still had short tails, there were two jolly tricksters who lived by guile and fraud. One of them wandered with his wife and tent in the Syr-Darya steppes, the other, in the steppes of Sary-Arka. Their fame spread far and wide, for people loved to talk about their clever tricks, and each heard many a good tale about the other.

One day the two decided, each by himself, that they must meet and test their skills to see who would outwit the other.

They greased their boots, stuffed the ends of their robes into their belts, and set out on the journey. They walked and walked, until they met one day on a caravan route near a newly built tomb. They embraced like old friends and sat down to converse a while.

"Any news?" asked the Syr-Darya trickster.

"Good news," replied the Sary-Arka trickster. "See

this new tomb? A famous bey was buried in it a short while ago. He left great herds of cattle and much gold, and all of it went to his half-wit son."

Said the Syr-Darya trickster:

"A bey won't give you what he has, and a poor man must look out for himself. . . . Let's see if we can get a hundred gold coins from the son and share it half and half."

And the Sary-Arka trickster said:

"May butter melt in your mouth! I agree. But how shall we do it?"

Two tricksters, two clever cheats—it was no trouble for them to devise a plan. They had a bite to eat, lit up their pipes, considered it a while, and came to a decision.

The Syr-Darya trickster climbed into the tomb and hid there, and the Sary-Arka man wrapped his head in the green turban of a wandering pilgrim and went to the mountain village to see the bey's son.

"My child," he said. "Some time ago your father borrowed a hundred gold pieces from me, and said: 'If I am alive, I will return them as soon as you demand them; if I am dead, my son will pay you.' It's time for me to collect the debt. Fulfill your father's promise."

The bey's son stared at him with an open mouth. It is easy to take, but it is difficult to give. After some thought, he said:

"And how will you prove to me that there is no deception in your words?"

The trickster sorrowfully shook his head and answered with a sigh:

"If my green turban means nothing to you, go to your father's grave; perhaps he will reveal to you the truth himself."

The young bey approached his father's tomb with fear and trembling, and asked:

"Father, is the pilgrim in the green turban telling me the truth about the hundred gold coins that you owe him?"

And the Syr-Darya trickster answered from the tomb in a booming, hollow voice:

"It is the truth, it is the truth, my son! I have been suffering great torment here because of this unpaid debt. Return the money to the holy man at once, and let my dead bones rest at last!"

In a cold sweat, the bey's son came running home, and without a word counted out a hundred gold coins.

The Sary-Arka trickster put the gold into his bosom and thought:

"Now let my friend sit in the tomb till he gets tired of it, and I will find my way home through the steppe."

Days and weeks went by. He returned to his tent, buried the gold under the hearth and gave his wife strict orders:

"If a Syr-Darya man comes here and asks for me, tell him that I died suddenly and was buried according to the law. Try to get rid of him as quickly as you can, and in the meantime bring my dinner every evening to the ravine. I shall be there until he goes."

Well, the Syr-Darya trickster waited for his friend in the dark tomb until he realized he had been fooled. He made his way out into the light, looked toward Sary-Arka, and said:

"The steppe is wide, but man is quick! You will not hide from me, good fellow. Just wait, my dove, and you'll fish out with your spoon exactly what you put into my pot!"

With these words he tightened his sash and set off in search of the swindler. He walked a day, he walked a week, he walked a month. And finally he found in the steppe the tent of the deceiver. He opened the door and stepped across the threshold.

As soon as she saw a stranger, the wife of the Sary-Arka trickster began to weep and wail:

"Oh, my unhappy husband! He died so suddenly! It's three days since we buried him. Whoever you may be, O stranger, leave me alone with my grief! . . ."

You're wasting time, dear woman, trying to forge cold iron, thought the Syr-Darya visitor. But aloud he said, tears gushing from his eyes:

"Woman, you break my heart with your tears. So my friend is dead! Oh, sorrow, sorrow! How can I leave the dwelling of the dead without mourning him? I promise to remain here forty years, until my eyes grow blind with weeping."

And, still sobbing, he settled down comfortably in the place of honor.

Day followed day, and the Syr-Darya trickster lived on in the tent, feasting in honor of his dead friend on the friend's own lamb and cheese. Nor did it escape his notice that the mistress of the house disappeared somewhere every evening with a full sack. One day he followed her stealthily and learned the road to the ravine.

A day came when the mistress was invited to visit friends. She dressed up in her best clothes and left for the whole day, returning only in the evening. The Syr-Darya trickster lost no time: he put on the woman's dress, filled a sack with food, and when darkness fell, he came down to the ravine to the Sary-Arka trickster. The latter did not notice the deception and greedily began to eat. Then he asked:

"Well, is that swindler showing any sign of leaving?"

Changing his voice, the Syr-Darya trickster said:

"No, he doesn't budge. He's still pretending he is crushed with sorrow, but all the time he's searching and sniffing around. You must have hidden something from him. I am afraid he'll find it."

The Sary-Arka man laughed:

"Don't worry, silly. He'll dry out like a woodbine stick before he finds anything. But just to be sure, keep an eye on the hearth. If you notice anything, let me know."

"Sure, I will," said the Syr-Darya wag, but to himself he thought: So that's it! He buried it under the hearth!

The mistress of the house came home and found the Syr-Darya trickster in his usual place, drinking mare's milk and shedding bitter tears. Hurriedly, she snatched the sack and ran to her husband, afraid he would scold her for coming so late.

When the Sary-Arka trickster saw his wife, he cried:

"What happened? Tell me, quick! Why did you come a second time?"

His wife said:

"May your life be long, dear husband, what is wrong with you? I wasn't here today."

"Oh, madwoman, you've ruined me!" cried her husband and rushed headlong to the tent.

But where the gold had been, there was nothing but the wind.

No wonder the old men say: "Don't brag of your strength, you'll find a stronger man; don't brag of your cunning, you'll find another still more cunning."

The Sary-Arka trickster thought a while, and said:

"Sometimes luck turns its face to us, sometimes its back. And he who gives himself to sorrow only feeds his troubles. It's only a fool who, angry at the lice, will throw his coat into the fire."

He bade farewell to his wife, mounted a hornless ox, and, urging him on with a knotty stick, set off for the Syr-Darya steppe.

While the Sary-Arka man was traveling through the steppe, asking the way of those he met, the Syr-Darya trickster got home and told his wife to announce to the whole village that he had died. He wrapped himself in a shroud and stretched out motionless, like a corpse. His wife obediently did everything he told her. When they heard her wailing, neighbors gathered, talked, wept, regretted his untimely death, then they carried him to a deserted tomb and returned to the tent for a mourning feast.

At the height of the feast, the Sary-Arka swindler rode up to the village on his hornless ox. When he heard what happened, he immediately said to himself: "Well, that's a familiar song." But he pretended sorrow at the dreadful news and cried out, sobbing:

"If my best and dearest friend is dead, I too will die. There is no happiness for me without him, for life without him is dark. I beg you one thing only—lay me down next to him, do not part us in death."

And with these words, he fell upon the ground, held his breath, and pretended to be dead. Without much delay, they picked him up and laid him to rest next to his friend.

After the people had gone, both swindlers remained in the tomb by themselves.

"Assalam-aleikum," said the Sary-Arka trickster quietly.

"Valeikum-as-salam," the Syr-Darya trickster answered just as quietly.

"Isn't it time for us to divide the bey's gold coins?"

"Well, maybe it is."

But as soon as they began to speak, there was a loud clattering of hooves and noise and ringing outside the tomb, and a band of robbers—forty desperate cutthroats—burst into the tomb.

Sitting down in a circle, the robbers began to share their spoils. Thirty-nine men were to get a pile of gold each, and the fortieth—an old sword. But none of the robbers would accept the sword. Everyone wanted gold. Then the leader of the band said:

"Fools, isn't a fine sword better than a handful of gold? With a sword, any brave man will defend himself and get more gold. And this old sword is fit for a great hero. Just watch how I'll chop those two corpses in half with a single blow!" and he pulled the sword out of its hilt.

Without waiting for trouble, the two tricksters in their white shrouds jumped up and shouted in terrifying voices:

"Black sinners, accursed bloodsuckers! It's not enough for you to make the living weep, you dare to raise your hand against the dead? Tremble! Beware! The hour of judgment is upon you!"

A wild panic broke out. Leaving all the wealth, the robbers leaped and jumped over one another toward the narrow door. Those who could not get out through the door dashed their heads and shoulders against the walls, broke through, and ran. In a few minutes they were a distance of three days' fast ride from the tomb.

The tricksters threw off their shrouds, divided all the treasures share and equal share like brothers, had a great good laugh, embraced, and each went off, still laughing, toward his own home.

MAYMUNYAK OR
THE MAGIC OF
THE YELLOW MONKEY

An Uygur Tale

A rich man had three sons. When they grew up, their father decided it was time for them to marry. He gave each son a bow and arrow and said:

"Shoot your arrows high, and see on whose roof they will fall. Then we shall send matchmakers to ask for the daughter of the house as your bride."

The eldest son's arrow fell on the roof of the khan's palace.

The arrow of the middle son fell on the roof of the house of the khan's vizier.

The youngest son, Pei, also pulled the bowstring and let his arrow fly. It rose and rose into the sky and disappeared from sight.

The two elder brothers, well pleased with themselves,

went home, and the youngest set off in search of his arrow.

He walked for many days, and finally came to the foot of a tall mountain covered with dense forest. Here he found his arrow, stuck in the earth. And next to it sat a yellow monkey.

The young man wondered at his fate, but he said: "Well, monkey, I suppose it is our destiny to live together and share the warmth of the same hearth."

And the monkey answered in a human voice:

"True, this is your fate." And, snatching up the arrow, she ran deeper into the woods, beckoning to the young man to come with her.

Obediently, the young man followed her.

For a long time they walked through the forest thickets, and suddenly they came to a palace wrought in gold and precious stones.

The young man stopped at the threshold, dazed with astonishment. But the monkey seized his hand and led him into the palace. She seated him in the place of honor and disappeared. A moment later, the door opened, and a maiden of untold beauty came into the room. She was more radiant than a fourteen-day-old moon.

"You thought yourself the unhappiest man, Pei, condemned to a lifetime with a monkey," said the maiden. "But your fate is not as cruel as you feared. I am not really a monkey. I am a peri, and I am your bride. But you must never tell anyone about it, or evil will befall."

The young man fell in love at first sight with his bride, whose name was Maymunyak.

Happily they lived together for days, weeks, and months. But after a time young Pei began to miss his home and parents. Nothing could quench his longing to see them. He grew thin and turned as yellow as saffron.

"What ails you?" asked his wife. "Why are you wasting away like this from day to day? Perhaps you miss your family and home?"

"I miss my native land, and I long to see my father and my mother."

"Very well," said Maymunyak. "I'll give you five days' time to visit your home and your parents."

"But they live far from here, and I don't know the way. I will not be able to get there and back in five days."

"That's easy, I will help you," said Maymunyak, and brought him a splendid horse.

"This horse will cover in a single day a distance it would take an ordinary horse a year to travel."

Pei mounted the magic horse, and in a day he was at home with his parents. There he learned that his elder brother had married the khan's daughter, and the middle brother had married the daughter of the vizier. The brothers' wives were ugly, clumsy as turtles, and, in addition, lazy and stupid. Whatever they turned to came out lopsided and wrong. But the brothers never noticed this, and were mightily pleased with their highborn wives.

"And what about your wife, brother Pei?" they asked. "What is she like?"

"I married a monkey," said Pei.

"And do you live with her in a great and beautiful palace?" the brothers mocked.

"The palace where we live is adorned with pure gold," said the younger son.

His brothers rolled with laughter and boasted about their rich and powerful relations.

The father heard all this. He called his sons together and said to them:

"It's time now to test the cleverness and skills of your young wives. Take these bags of flour, and let each one bake me pastries of forty-one kinds for tomorrow."

The elder brothers ran to urge their wives to hurry, and Pei mounted his horse and sadly rode back to the mountains. He was certain that his Maymunyak would not be able to fulfill his father's request, since she was not familiar with human ways.

When he came home, he placed the flour before Maymunyak and told her of his father's order.

"Don't worry, this is simple," Maymunyak said to him. "Walk toward those mountains, to the right, until you see a house, then shout into the first window on the left: 'Hundziak, Kundziak, Maymunyak wants you! Then you must return without looking back."

Pei did everything she told him, and when he came home he saw two lovely maidens, so like Maymunyak that it was difficult to tell them apart. Rays of light spread from their faces, and the palace was even brighter than ever.

After the girls laughed, and spoke, and played their fill, Maymunyak said to them:

"Hundziak, Kundziak, go into the yard and build me a large open stove. Then make a fire in it."

Then she took the flour, poured it into the stove, sprinkled it with water, and covered the stove.

"And now," she said, "it's time to go to bed."

In the morning Pei found before him a tray with pastries of forty-one kinds, each looking more delectable than the next. He put them in a sack and took them to his father.

His father was delighted with the pastries. But the wives of his other sons were only just beginning to sift the flour. When they learned that Maymunyak had already completed her task, they begged Pei to tell them how she had done it.

They also ordered open stoves built in their yards, poured the flour into them, sprinkled it with water, closed the stoves, and went to bed.

In the morning they could just scrape out the burnt dough, and they sent it with their husbands to their father-in-law. The old man looked at it and spat.

On the following day he called his sons together again and, giving each a piece of silk, said:

"Let your wives make new dresses for themselves by morning."

The elder brothers took the silk and ran to their wives, and the youngest rode home. He gave the silk to Maymunyak and told her of his father's request.

Maymunyak called the girls again. They cut the silk into tiny shreds, bound it into a kerchief, and put it in the corner.

In the morning, when Pei was ready to return to his father, Maymunyak untied the kerchief and took out a dress so skillfully made that it did not have a single seam.

The youth took the dress and rode off to his homeland. As he approached his father's house, his brothers' wives ran out to meet him. They had not even started the work and did not know how to go about it. Seeing the dress made by Maymunyak, they begged Pei to tell them how she had done it.

Then the women hurried home, seized the silk, cut it into shreds, tied them into kerchiefs and put the bundles in a corner. In the morning, sure that the dresses were ready, they did not even trouble to untie the kerchiefs and sent them to their father-in-law.

When he saw what the women had done with the silk, he merely gasped. But the dress made by Maymunyak pleased him so much that he decided to test his sons' wives a third time.

He gave each son a bundle of cotton wool and said:

"Let your wives spin me cotton thread of forty-one kinds, of different thicknesses and different colors. I give them till tomorrow to complete this task."

Pei brought the cotton wool home and told Maymunyak what his father had requested.

Maymunyak went to the barn and stuffed the cotton wool into her buffalo's mouth. In the morning they came and found at his feet forty-one skeins of thread of different thicknesses and different colors.

The brothers' wives again met Pei and asked him how Maymunyak had spun and dyed and dried so much cotton in a single day. The young man told them what she had done.

The women seized the cotton wool, ran to their barns, and stuffed it into the mouths of their buffaloes. In the morning they came and found that the beasts had died of suffocation.

After this, the father decided that the wives of his elder sons were hopelessly stupid, and he said so to his sons.

The elder brothers and their wives conceived a bitter hatred for Maymunyak.

And the old man thought: Pei's wife must possess some magic powers. It is time I met her myself.

He invited all his sons to visit him three days later and to bring their wives.

On the appointed day the younger son, together with

his wife Maymunyak and her two lovely friends, rode up to the father's house on magnificent white horses.

The old people welcomed Maymunyak and set her in the place of honor.

After a while, the mother-in-law asked her sons' wives to help her prepare the meal for the invited guests, and bid each of them watch one of the pots. In Maymunyak's pot everything was quickly boiled and cooked without fire or smoke. But her sisters-in-law had no end of trouble. Either the fire would not light, or the wood would not burn, or the pot ran over. And they brought the food to the table half raw and half burnt.

The guests just barely managed, for politeness's sake, to swallow the tasteless food. Then everyone began to dance and make merry. Maymunyak danced so beautifully that no one could take his eyes away from her. The youngest wife enchanted everyone, and all the guests had nothing but praise for her. The wives of the older brothers turned black with envy and vowed to avenge themselves on the young girl and her husband.

Maymunyak and her friends went home after the feast, and Pei remained with his parents for a few more days.

The brothers' wives called Pei and began to speak to him in their sweetest tones:

"You are our kinsman," they said, "and we wish you no evil. But we are older than you, and you must listen to us and do everything we say. Your wife has an old yellow dress that she wears all the time. Why does she need it if she is such a skillful dressmaker? Take that dress and burn it, and throw the ashes into the river. Then your Maymunyak will always wear beautiful new dresses that will make her still lovelier."

Pei promised to do as they suggested, and they rejoiced, for they suspected that there was some magic in the yellow dress.

When Pei came home, he said nothing of all this to Maymunyak. At night, when she was sleeping, he found her old yellow dress and burned it in the fire and threw the ashes into the river.

In the morning Maymunyak searched and searched for the dress everywhere, and finally she asked her husband:

"Have you seen my yellow dress?"

"Yes," he said, "but it was so old and shabby that I burned it. Why don't you wear your beautiful new dresses instead?"

"You burned it!" she cried. "And what did you do with the ashes?"

"I threw them into the river."

"Oh, what have you done!" cried Maymunyak and clapped her hands in sorrow. "Under the yellow dress I had my monkey skin. I had to wear it only until the next new moon, and then I would be human forever. Now I don't know when this time will come, and I must leave you at once. If you truly love me and wish to find me, make yourself seven pairs of iron boots and three iron staffs, then travel east. When you wear out the seven pairs of iron boots and your three iron staffs, you will come to the region where I must live until then."

With these words Maymunyak called her friends; they all turned into bats and flew away. The golden palace vanished, and Pei found himself alone in the dense forest.

His grief knew no bounds. But, knowing that tears would never bring back his Maymunyak, he set to work. He forged himself seven pairs of iron boots and three iron staffs. Then he started walking east to look for Maymunyak.

He crossed waterless deserts, made his way through trackless forests, climbed high mountains. He went on and on. He managed to cross dangerous swamps and quicksands and snowy mountain passes. And finally he wore out the seven pairs of iron boots and the three iron staffs. Weary, hungry, and barefoot, he approached the highest mountain he had ever seen and sat down by a mountain spring that flowed from a cleft in the rock.

"Can I go on?" he asked himself despairingly. "Should I go on?" The way looked hopeless, and he decided that there was only one road left to him: the shortest road—to death.

Suddenly the young man heard footsteps and a crashing of branches. He jumped and looked around. A hideous old woman was hobbling to the spring for water.

"Hey! Who is here?" she shouted.

"I, a man," said Pei.

"If you're a man, I will have a fine supper tonight," said the woman, seized his hand with her crooked fingers, and pulled him after her.

The young man did not care what happened to him any longer, and he followed her without resisting.

She brought him to the ruins of an old mill in a dried riverbed. Here she gave the young man an axe, pointed to a gnarled, knotty tree trunk, and said:

"You must split this log with one blow into forty-one pieces. If you don't, I'll eat you."

Pei looked at the old, nicked, rusty axe, thinking that with such an axe you could not even make a dent in the century-old tree trunk, let alone split it into forty-one pieces. Well, he thought to himself, I see that my end is really near. Suddenly he heard the voice of Maymunyak.

She told him that the hideous old crone was a yalmauz —a terrible man-eating witch, and that the yalmauz was her stepmother. She had bewitched even Maymunyak's father, who was himself a mighty div, a skilled wizard, and made him promise to kill Maymunyak.

"Listen carefully," said Maymunyak, "and do all that I say: Strike the trunk and cry out: 'O-oh! By the magic of the yellow monkey!' And the witch's bidding will be done. Meantime, my friends and I will think of a plan to save you and escape from here."

The young man did as she said, and the log split into forty-one pieces.

The yalmauz came out and raged to see her orders carried out. Then she gave Pei a small needle and pointed to the old mill. "With this needle," she said, "you must bring the water back under the wheels, so they will turn again and work the mill. If you don't do it, you will die." And she went back into the house.

Pei stuck the needle into the dry ground under the wheels and cried: "O-oh! By the magic of the yellow monkey!" And at once fresh water flowed along the riverbed, the wheels began to turn, and the millstones ground the grain into flour.

The old witch realized that someone must be helping Pei and locked him in the cellar.

Maymunyak and her friends decided it was time to save her husband and to flee. But to do this, she had to outwit her evil stepmother. The girls turned into quail, flew to the window of the cellar where the young man was imprisoned, and flapped their wings. And suddenly Pei felt that he had also grown wings. As a gray quail, he dashed out of the barred window, and all of them flew as fast as they could from the accursed spot.

As soon as the yalmauz learned that her stepdaughter and the young man were gone, she turned into a crow and tried to overtake them. But she fell far behind. Then she returned, wakened her sleeping husband, the old

div, turned him into a hawk and sent him in pursuit of the four fugitives.

Maymunyak soon felt that her father was gaining upon them. Alighting in a melon field, she turned her husband into a melon, her friends into sacks, and herself into an old watchman.

Her father came to the melon field, alighted, and, assuming the likeness of a traveler, he went up to the watchman and asked:

"Have you seen four people pass here recently?"

"No, I haven't," said the watchman.

The traveler vanished, and a hawk rose from the field and flew in the opposite direction. Maymunyak turned herself and her companions into wild geese, and they flew on.

But her father soon guessed that she had outwitted him. He turned back and started catching up with them again. Then Maymunyak turned her friends into dried cow dung, which in those woodless regions was used as fuel; she turned her husband into a sack, and herself into an old woman gathering the dung into the sack.

When her father came flying, he turned into an old man and asked whether the woman had seen four people passing by. She said she had not, and her father, turned into a falcon, flew in the opposite direction.

A small flock of birds rose up again into the sky. At the very house of Pei's father, the falcon caught up with them, and wanted to snatch Maymunyak. But at this moment, she dropped upon the old, moss-grown gates and turned into a beautiful, wide-open yellow flower.

The other birds flew into the yard and sat down in a tree, waiting, for they could do nothing to help Maymunyak.

Her father turned into an old beggar and walked up to the master of the house, Pei's father, who was standing in the doorway, to ask for alms. The master offered him bread, but he refused. His servants brought out some old clothing, but the beggar refused again. He was offered money, but he did not want that either.

"What is it you want, then?" asked Pei's father.

"Give me that flower blooming on your old gates!"

Pei's father marveled at this strange request, but permitted the beggar to pluck the flower. However, as soon as the old man began to climb up the gate, the flower dropped and scattered into a handful of rice.

A rooster jumped down from the gate and quickly began to peck the rice. He pecked up all the grains except for one, which had fallen into a crack under the gate. The rooster turned back into the beggar.

"That's done!" he said, and turned to go. But at that moment the last grain of rice rolled out from under the gate and turned into Maymunyak, who cried to the old man:

"Well, father, you see, I outwitted you after all. Now you have no more power over me, and I'll remain a human being all my life."

The old beggar said nothing, bowed low, stepped out of the gates, and disappeared forever.

Now Pei and the two maidens resumed their human shapes. They embraced Maymunyak, and all of them were welcomed and went to live in the house of Pei's kind parents. After a time, the girls also found fine and brave young husbands. The days of human life that were allotted to each of them were spent in peace and plenty.

They remained in Pei's homeland, and I have come here to you to tell their story.

THE WISE NASREDDIN

An Uygur Tale

 man asked wise Nasreddin:
"Tell me, wise teacher, when the new moon is born, what happens to the old?"

Nasreddin answered:

"When a new moon is born, God chops the old one into stars."

Nasreddin saw a thief in his house and quickly climbed into a trunk.

"Why are you hiding there?" asked the thief when he opened the trunk.

"There's nothing worth stealing in my house. I am ashamed of my poverty."

Nasreddin always had a witty answer for everything. Wait, thought his friend, I'll ask him a question that even he will not be able to answer. And he said to him:

"Teacher, what shall I do? I accidentally swallowed a live mouse. How can I get rid of it?"

"Swallow a cat!"

A man came to visit Nasreddin and did not find him home. Annoyed, he wrote "Ass" on his door and left.

A few days later Nasreddin met this friend and said:

"I'm sorry you did not find me home when you came."

"But how did you know it was I who came to see you?"

"My good friend," said Nasreddin, "you signed your name on the door."

A man asked Nasreddin:

"If the sea catches fire, where will the fish go?"

"They'll climb the trees," Nasreddin answered.

THE CLEVER WIFE

A Kirghiz Tale

long time ago there lived a khan called Sarybay.

One day he gathered his people and said to them:

"I have been your khan for forty years. I have seen a great deal in my lifetime. I have eaten and drunk all that has been assigned to me as my portion. Now the only thing left for me is to die. But I have no children, and there is no one to inherit the throne. Elect your own khan."

And the people replied to Sarybay:

"No, appoint a new khan for us yourself!"

But the khan said:

"The living soon forget the words of the dead. I will die, and my words will die with me."

Now, the people loved the khan, for he had been just and good, and they begged him again:

"We honor you and we honor your words. Appoint a new khan, and we shall accept him."

Then Sarybay said:

"I have a faithful friend—a white falcon. After I die

he will neither eat, nor drink, nor move for three days. On the fourth day, approach him, give him food and drink, and set him free. Watch closely where he goes. After a while he will alight on a man's head. That man should be your khan."

A week later Sarybay was dead. And his true friend, the white falcon, neither ate, nor drank, nor moved for three days. On the fourth day he was given food and drink, and then he was set free. The falcon rose high, circled round and round over the gathered people, and alighted on the head of a young shepherd, Bolotbek. There was great commotion. Some people shouted:

"Bolotbek is much too young. How can he rule the land?"

Others cried:

"We shall not bow to a simple shepherd as our khan!"

But the white-bearded elders stepped forward and addressed the people:

"We promised Sarybay to abide by the choice of the falcon. The falcon has chosen, and this young shepherd must be our khan."

And so Bolotbek became the khan of the land. He was wise and kind. He helped the poor and gave them cattle and clothing from the khan's own herds and storehouses. And his subjects loved and revered their khan.

Khan Bolotbek ruled long and justly. But one thing grieved the people: he did not take himself a wife. None of the lovely, proud daughters of beys and khans seemed to please him. And one day the elders came to him and begged him to marry.

"Remember Sarybay," they said. "He died without heirs, and you will, too, unless you take a wife."

For a long time they pleaded with him, and finally the khan consented.

"Very well," he said. "Call to me all the wellborn maidens in our khanate. I will ask them three riddles. The one who gives me the right answers will be my wife."

And all the highborn maidens of the khanate gathered in the palace. Bolotbek came out to them and asked them three riddles:

"What is the distance between the east and west?

"What is the distance between the earth and the sky?

"What is the distance between truth and falsehood?"

The khan gave them three days, and bade them come to the palace every morning and every evening and tell him what their answers were.

Two days went by, but none of the maidens found the answers to the khan's riddles. On the third day, as they were coming to the palace, they met a poor girl gathering firewood. The girl, whose name was Danyshman, asked them:

"Sisters, I see you going to the palace for the third day. Won't you tell me why?"

"It's none of your affair," the highborn maidens answered. "Your job is to gather firewood, not to ask questions."

But one of them was kinder and told her everything. Then Danyshman begged to be taken to the palace too. The maidens mocked her shabby dress and laughed at her, but finally agreed to take her with them. When they arrived at the palace, Khan Bolotbek asked:

"Well, which of you has guessed the answers to my riddles?"

None of the maidens answered. Then Danyshman stepped forward and said:

"I have the answers to your riddles, O khan. The distance between east and west is one day's journey, for in the morning the sun starts on its journey in the east, and in the evening it ends it in the west. The distance between the sky and earth is very small—it is easily encompassed with the eye: you raise your eyes and see the sky; you lower them, and see the earth. The third riddle is also simple. The distance between truth and falsehood is the width of no more than four fingers: it is the distance between the ear and the eye, for the ear often hears falsehood, but the eye always sees the truth."

"Right!" cried the khan. "You alone have found the answers to my riddles. You are the wisest maiden in the land, and I will marry you."

Bolotbek called the people to a wedding feast, and the poor girl became the khan's wife. They lived happily together. Both remembered their days of poverty and helped the poor. And Danyshman assisted the khan with her clever suggestions. For it was not for nothing that her name was Danyshman, which means "wise." The khan always listened to his wife, but he made her promise that she would never give advice and share her wisdom with anyone but him.

One day a young man committed a grievous offense, for which the punishment was death. He came to the khan's wife and implored her to teach him how to escape the inevitable penalty.

Danyshman took pity on him and broke the word she had given her husband. She told the young man what answers to give the khan on judgment day.

"But do not tell the khan I taught you," she warned him.

However, Khan Bolotbek saw at once that the young man could not have thought of such clever answers himself, and began to question him:

"Tell me who advised you! If you do not tell me, you shall die!"

The frightened young man confessed that Danyshman had taught him what to say. The khan flew into a rage. He strode into his wife's apartments and he cried:

"You have not kept your word. That means you cannot be a faithful wife to me! Until this day we have lived in love and harmony, but now you must leave my palace and my city. Go! The only thing I'll grant you is permission to take with you whatever is most precious to you in the palace."

"Very well," said Danyshman. "I'll go, but I will make

a single request: Dine with me for the last time before I leave."

And Bolotbek agreed.

The khan's wife prepared a fine meal, brought wine, and served her husband. When the khan had had his fill of food and drink, he fell asleep. Danyshman ordered the best horses to be harnessed to a cart. She put her sleeping husband into the cart, whipped the horses, and drove away as fast as they could go.

Soon they arrived in another khanate. Bolotbek woke up and looked around, and discovered that he was in a strange city. And next to him he saw his wife Danyshman.

Khan Bolotbek cried out in dismay:

"What is the meaning of this? What have you done to me?"

"My khan," replied his wife. "You told me: 'Leave my palace and my city. Go! But I permit you to take with you whatever is most precious to you.' I left your palace, I left your city, but I took you with me, for you are more precious to me than anything or anyone in the whole world."

Bolotbek hung his head in shame before his clever wife, for he understood that he had been unjust. And so they both returned to their palace, and spent the rest of their days, as formerly, in peace and happiness.

THE SHEPHERD,
THE TIGER,
AND THE FOX

A Kirghiz Tale

 shepherd brought his sheep into the field to graze, and sat down under a tree to rest. Suddenly a tiger came out of the woods.

The shepherd picked up his staff and jumped up.

The tiger was just about to spring at the man when he saw the staff and got frightened. He thought it was a gun. They stared at each other, and neither dared to make the first move.

At that moment, a fox came running by. He saw that the tiger and the shepherd were afraid of each other and decided to turn the situation to his own advantage.

He ran up to the tiger and said:

"Cousin tiger, there is no reason to be afraid of a man. Jump on him, get him down, and have a good meal."

"You're cunning," growled the tiger, "but you have no

brains. Look at him—he has a gun. He'll fire, and that will be the end of me. Be off with your stupid advice."

"Well, if that's the case, I'll go and ask him not to shoot you. What will you give me if I save you?"

"Anything you ask."

The fox ran to the shepherd and said:

"Uncle shepherd, why are you standing here? The tiger wants to make a meal of you. I just persuaded him to wait a while. What will you give me if I save you?"

And the shepherd promised:

"Anything you ask."

The fox ran to the tiger and said:

"Cousin tiger, you'll have a long life. I just persuaded the shepherd not to shoot you. Hurry up and run now! I'll see you later. If he gets angry again, he'll fire his gun and it will be the end of you."

The tiger turned and leaped away as fast as he could go.

And the fox came back to the shepherd.

"Uncle shepherd, you did not forget your promise?"

"No," said the shepherd. "Tell me what you want."

"I don't want much, only a bite out of your leg. That will be enough for me."

The shepherd stretched out his leg. But just as the fox was about to sink his teeth into it, the shepherd screamed. The fox jumped back.

"Who made that noise?"

"What do you care? Take your bite, and be done with it!"

"Oh, no! I won't come near you before you tell me who made that noise," said the frightened fox.

"In that case, I will tell you," answered the shepherd. "Last year we had a bad winter in the village. We had nothing to eat. And then my sheep dog had two puppies. Well . . . I was so hungry, I ate them. Now the pups have grown up in my stomach. I guess they smell you and want to get at you, so they are barking."

The fox got even more frightened, but he would not show it. He said with dignity:

"I'd have no trouble handling your pups. But I must run and see the tiger on some urgent business. Hold back your sheep dogs for a while. When I come back, I'll teach them such a lesson that they will never attack foxes again."

"Very well, make it quick," said the shepherd.

And the fox went streaking off into the woods, happy to get away with his life.

After he caught his breath, he set out to look for the tiger: perhaps he would have better luck with him.

"Well, cousin tiger," the fox said when he found him. "I saved your life when you were frightened of the shepherd, and you made a promise. Now you must keep it!"

"What promise?" roared the tiger. "I am no cousin to you. I am the shah of these woods. Who dares to say that I was frightened?"

And he raised his paw to strike the fox down.

"There is no gratitude in this world," the fox said to himself, and slunk into his hole to teach his children to stay away from men and tigers.

THE KAHA BIRD

A Tadzhik Tale

nce upon a time there lived an old fisherman. Early in the morning he would go down to the river and sit there fishing all day. And in the evening, when he counted his catch, there never would be more than a fish or two. He sold the fish in the market and bought a little food for himself and his wife. And almost every day they went to bed half hungry.

One morning he went down to the river to fish, when suddenly a beautiful great bird with shiny silver plumage flew in from somewhere and sat down on the tree above him. This was not an ordinary bird—it was the magical Kaha bird herself, who often helped poor people when they were in trouble.

The Kaha watched the fisherman as he waited and waited until he caught a tiny little fish. Then she asked him:

"What will you do with this fish, grandpa?"

"I'll take it to market and sell it, so I can buy a piece of bread for myself and my old wife."

The bird took pity on the old man.

"You have worked and suffered long enough," she said to him. "I shall bring you a big fish every night. You will get a lot of money for it, and you and your wife won't have to live in poverty any more."

At midnight the Kaha bird came flying with a large fish and dropped it in the old man's yard.

In the morning the old fisherman cut the big fish into pieces, fried them and took them to the market to sell.

From that day on the Kaha bird came every night and brought the old man a big fish. Little by little the old man, who had been so poor, became quite rich, and even bought himself a house with a garden.

One day, when he brought his fish to market, he heard the crier of the shah himself shouting for all to hear:

"Our shah has heard about a marvelous, magical Kaha bird. Whoever tells him where to find this bird will get half of his kingdom and fifty bags of gold."

The old man jumped up from his place to tell the crier that he knew where the bird could be found. But then he thought: "This bird has saved me from poverty and hunger. How can I betray her?" And he sat down again.

"Still," he said to himself, "it would be nice to be the lord of half the kingdom," and he stood up again.

And so he argued with himself, getting up and sitting down, getting up and sitting down, until the crier saw him and dragged the old man to the palace, before the shah himself.

"This old man knows where to find the Kaha bird!" he cried.

And the shah said to the fisherman:

"If you know about the Kaha bird, tell me where to find her. I've grown blind, and no known remedies have helped me. But a wise healer from a distant land has told me that if I wash my eyes in the blood of the Kaha bird, I will regain my sight at once. Help me to find the bird, and I will give you half my kingdom and fifty bags of gold!"

And the old man, overcome with greed, said:

"Mighty Shah, the Kaha bird comes to my yard at midnight every night and brings me a big fish."

The shah rejoiced and told him:

"Well, then, you must catch her for me!"

But the old man said:

"No, the Kaha bird is large and strong. I'll never be able to catch her myself. To catch and hold her will take more than a hundred men."

"I'll send four hundred of my servants with you," said the shah. "Hide them under the tree where the bird sits down. They will know how to catch and hold her.

"No," said the old man. "You cannot catch her that way. You can't use force, you must be cunning. When she comes to me, I shall prepare a feast and then per-

suade her to come down on earth. Then we shall catch
her."

The shah sent four hundred servants with the fisherman. He hid them under the branches of the tree where
the Kaha bird always alighted. The servants sat and
waited, without moving hand or foot.

And the old man spread a rug near the tree and set
out all sorts of delicacies to tempt the Kaha bird. As
soon as the bird came, he spoke to her:

"My dear friend, dear Kaha bird! Thanks to you I
have grown rich and happy, and yet I've never even
asked you to dine with me. Come down and do me the
honor of sharing my meal!"

At first the Kaha bird refused, but he begged her so
sweetly and so cunningly, that she began to waver. For
a moment she wondered: "Why is he begging me so
much? What if he has some evil thing in mind?" But
then she answered herself: "What can he do to me, he is
so old and weak! Besides, I have done him so much
good." And so, ashamed of her suspicions, she came
down from the tree and sat down on the rug next to the
old man.

He set all the fine dishes before her:

"My dearest friend, beloved Kaha! Eat! Try this, and
now try that! I have prepared it all myself with love
and gratitude!"

But as soon as the Kaha bird began to peck at the

food in the dish, he caught her by the feet and cried:

"I have her! Come out, come out, quick!"

The shah's four hundred servants leaped out and rushed toward the bird. But the huge bird merely spread her wings and rose into the air, with the old man hanging onto her feet and shouting: "I have her, I have her!"

Then one of the shah's servants jumped up and caught the old man's feet to pull them down. But he, too, rose above the ground. A second servant caught him by the feet. A third caught the second. A fourth caught the third. A fifth caught the fourth, until the old man and

all the shah's four hundred servants hung by one another's feet, while the Kaha bird rose higher and higher,
right up into the clouds.

At this moment, the old man looked down, but he
could no longer see the earth. "Oh-h!" he cried and
everything turned dark before his eyes. His fingers
loosed their hold on the bird's feet, and he plunged down
and down and down. And with him, all the shah's four
hundred servants. Down they came and smashed themselves to bits.

And the magical great Kaha bird returned to her kingdom in the clouds, and no man ever saw her again.

THE BEAR'S SON

An Uzbek Tale

 nce upon a time the great city of Tashkent was ruled by a khan called Eron. For a long time he had no children, which caused him endless grief. At long last a son was born to him, and he named him Jekovoy.

The khan loved his son and took him along wherever he went.

One day he went out hunting in the valley of Chinaz and took his young son with him. Suddenly a huge she-bear jumped out of the reeds, seized the boy, and carried him off. Khan Eron and his hunters galloped in pursuit, but the she-bear disappeared. For forty days and forty nights the inconsolable khan searched for his son, but never found him.

Now, listen about the khan's son.

When she seized the boy, the she-bear took him to her den. Every day she went out hunting and brought him food.

Years went by. The boy grew into a tall, strong youth. He came to love the she-bear and considered her his mother. Now they always hunted together. And the young man became bearlike, himself. His body was covered with thick fur, and his voice was like a bear's roar.

One day Khan Eron went out hunting again in the Chinaz and met a huge she-bear. Without a moment's thought, he shot an arrow at her and killed her on the spot.

At that moment a tall young man leaped out of the reeds. He raised his spear and shouted in rage:

"Who are you? How did you dare to kill my mother?"

Khan Eron stopped, astonished at the young man's beauty.

"How can a beast be a man's mother?" he asked.

"The she-bear fed and raised me. To me she was a mother, and I shall avenge her death."

He was about to plunge his spear into the khan when Eron said:

"Stop, or you will be the murderer of your own father. You are my son Jekovoy. The she-bear stole you many years ago and I mourned you as dead. I grieved for years, but now I rejoice to find that you're alive. Come to me and let me embrace you, my newfound son!"

They embraced and returned to Tashkent.

The khan ordered a great feast to celebrate his son's return, and assigned to Jekovoy the best apartments in the palace.

But Jekovoy still grieved for his adopted mother-bear and finally obtained the khan's permission to return to his native region of Chinaz.

Jekovoy came to the den where he had grown up, and he wept and said aloud:

"Oh, my mother, see how I mourn for you. But since your murderer is my own father, how can I avenge your death?"

The khan had in the meantime sent out spies to see what his son was doing in Chinaz. One of the spies heard Jekovoy's last words and immediately reported to the khan that his son was plotting to avenge the murder of the she-bear.

The khan was very frightened, and he said:

"After all, he is half a man and half a beast. He will surely kill me. What shall I do?"

And he sent a servant to his son with the command:

"My son, go to the Chinaz bogs, chop down many trees for firewood. I shall soon pay you a visit with my entire court, and we shall have a feast and celebration."

Secretly, Khan Eron hoped that his son would be attacked and torn to pieces by the wild beasts who lived in the bog.

But Jekovoy went out into his native woods and gave a loud call. A thousand tigers, a thousand bears, a thousand wolves, a thousand foxes, and a thousand birds gathered in answer to his call. They bowed to the young man and asked:

"O Son of the She-Bear, what do you wish?"

"Gather me a mountain-high pile of firewood."

When the wood was gathered, Jekovoy mounted the biggest tiger and said:

"Each of you, take all the wood that you can carry, and follow me." And all the beasts loaded the wood upon their backs and followed Jekovoy. Even the birds flew with them, carrying a twig or two in their beaks.

Jekovoy led them not to Chinaz, but straight to Tash-kent.

When they approached the city, the guards patrolling

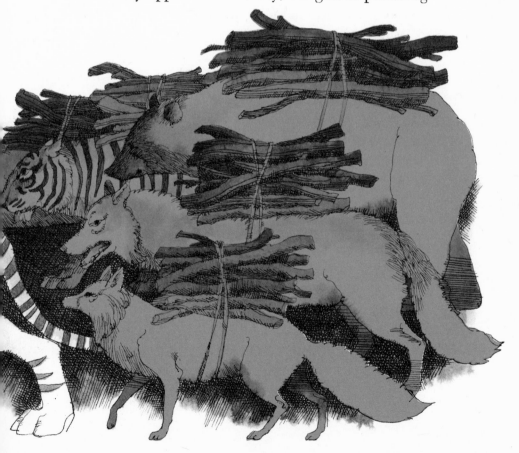

the walls ran frightened to Khan Eron and reported:

"All the wild beasts of the world are coming to make war on us. And your son, mounted on a tiger, is leading them."

"Ob-bo!" cried the terrified khan. "Our end is come."

And he sent out his vizier to Jekovoy with orders to pile up the wood outside the city walls.

The young man obeyed, and when the wood was stacked, he thanked the beasts and sent them home to the Chinaz bog with strict instructions not to harm any of the peasants or herdsmen they met on the way.

The khan gathered his viziers and asked them:

"What shall we do now?"

Then the eldest vizier suggested:

"The city of Chimkent belonged to you, great khan, but evil enemies took it away. Send your son to win the city back for you. If he wins it, good. If he perishes, still better."

Khan Eron called his son:

"You are a grown man now. It's time for you to prove your skills as a warrior. Go to Chimkent and win it back for me."

Jekovoy bowed his head, accepting the command.

"And how many soldiers will you need to go with you?" Khan Eron asked him.

The young man bowed again and said:

"I don't need any soldiers, but tell your blacksmiths to forge me a sword weighing seventy thousand pounds, and a hammer weighing sixteen thousand pounds."

They collected steel and iron from the whole land and summoned all the blacksmiths of Tashkent. For forty days and forty nights the blacksmiths toiled without rest, and forged for Jekovoy a sword and hammer so heavy that all the khan's warriors together could not lift them from the ground.

When Jekovoy came, he lifted up the sword with one hand and said:

"It's kind of light, but it will do!"

He swung it in the air once or twice, then stuck it inside his belt.

With the other hand he seized the hammer, twirled it around his head seven times, and stuck it also in his belt.

Then Jekovoy set out on the journey to Chimkent.

At that time the Chimkent fortress held an army of eighty thousand alien warriors, armed from head to foot.

Jekovoy walked up to the fortress wall and gave a shout. From his shout, forty thousand warriors dropped dead at once with fright. Jekovoy gave another shout. Thirty thousand other warriors said farewell to life. Jekovoy shouted a third time, and the last ten thousand warriors fell dead.

Jekovoy entered the Chimkent fortress and saw that there was nobody to fight.

In the nearby mountains poor Chimkent families were hiding, afraid of the enemy soldiers. Jekovoy caught sight of them and cried:

"Come back to Chimkent, all of you! From now on we shall live in peace and safety."

When Khan Eron heard about it, he turned purple with rage and summoned his viziers.

"What shall we do now?" he asked them.

And the eldest vizier said:

"Your son Jekovoy is spoiling the people. He lets them live too well and gives them too much freedom. Send him to the Tyan-Shan Mountains. Three giants live there—Tash Palvan, Kyrs Palvan, and Cedar Palvan. Tell Jekovoy to conquer the giants and bring them bound to Tashkent. If he succeeds, good. If he perishes, still better."

The khan sent orders to Jekovoy to conquer the giants and bring them to Tashkent.

Jekovoy began to make ready for the journey, and the people of Chimkent cried bitterly:

"You'll leave us, Jekovoy, and some evil khan will seize our city again and compel us to till the land for him and pay him taxes forty times a year."

"If I ever hear of such a thing, I shall come back," answered Jekovoy, "and turn the enemy to dust and ashes."

Jekovoy bid the people of Chimkent good-bye and went off to the Tyan-Shan Mountains. Who knows how long he walked, but after many days he met a giant carrying a huge mountain in each hand.

The young man asked the giant:

"Who are you, and where are you going?"

"My name is Tash Palvan, and I am going to Chimkent. I've heard of a certain Jekovoy, who came there and walks about with his nose up in the air. I want to beat him and become the ruler of Chimkent."

Jekovoy smiled and said:

"Why go to Chimkent? Fight me. I am a pupil of Jekovoy. If you beat me, then you will beat him too."

They began to wrestle. Jekovoy seized Tash Palvan by his belt and flung him, together with his two mountains, in a single throw over seven mountain tops.

Jekovoy strode over the seven mountains and found Tash Palvan half dead. He brought him water, and when the giant recovered a little, the young man asked him:

"Well, do you still want to go to Chimkent and fight Jekovoy?"

Tash Palvan rose with an effort from the ground, bowed low, kissed Jekovoy's hand, and said:

"If this is the pupil, what must the teacher be like? I will not go to Chimkent. Take me with you. I shall serve you and cook your lunch and dinner."

"Very well. But you must know that I am Jekovoy."

And they went on together.

After a time they met a second giant, who carried in each hand a mountain five times larger than the mountains of Tash Palvan. And he was throwing the mountains up and down like pebbles.

"Who are you, and where are you going?" asked Jekovoy.

"My name is Kyrs Palvan. I am going to conquer Chimkent and give a thrashing to some upstart named Jekovoy."

Jekovoy smiled and said:

"Why go so far? Try to give me a thrashing—I am Jekovoy's pupil. If you beat me, you will beat him too."

Kyrs Palvan looked at him with a contemptuous grin. But Jekovoy seized him by the collar of his robe and threw him up with his two mountains. Then he caught him and threw him up again. Then he caught him and threw him up a third time.

At this point Kyrs Palvan cried to him:

"Have mercy! I will not go to Chimkent, if Jekovoy has pupils like you. Allow me to be your servant."

Jekovoy agreed and told him who he was. Then he went on and the giants followed, helping him along the way.

Soon after that they met another giant. In each hand he held a thousand-year-old tree and played with them, throwing them up like splinters to the very sky.

"Who are you and where are you going?" asked Jekovoy.

"My name is Cedar Palvan. I am going to Chimkent. I want to make Jekovoy a present of these trees. If he accepts them, I will be his friend. If he rejects them, I will have a trial of strength with him."

"Don't go to Chimkent. Jekovoy will not accept your present. I am his pupil; have a trial of strength with me."

They began to play and wrestle. Jekovoy lifted up Cedar Palvan by the belt and threw him up to the very sky. For seven hours there was no sight of the giant. Seven hours later Jekovoy caught Cedar Palvan as he came flying down and asked:

"Well, will you go to Chimkent to fight Jekovoy?"

"Oh, no," cried Cedar Palvan, pale with fright. "Take me with you. Perhaps I can be useful to you in some way."

Jekovoy told him who he was, and they went on together.

In the evening they came to a mountain village. In a square in the middle of the village sat seven frightful witches—seven yalmauz—in a row. Before each one there was a fire, and suspended over each fire was an enormous cauldron with forty handles, and in each cauldron forty sheep were being stewed for the witches' supper.

"Salom, grandmothers," said Jekovoy.

And all the witches shouted in chorus:

"It's your good luck, young man, that you have greeted us, or else we would have gobbled you up at once, together with your giants! Now we shall leave you for tomorrow's supper."

Jekovoy was angered at these boastful words. He raised his hammer and gave the first witch such a blow on the head that her head flew off her shoulders and struck the head of the second witch. The second head flew off and struck the third one. The third one flew off and struck the fourth, till all the witches' heads flew off their shoulders.

When the stew in the cauldrons was ready, Jekovoy said to his giants:

"If you are hungry, eat."

The giants ate and ate, and all the three together could not finish the stew even in a single cauldron.

And Jekovoy said to them:

"If you cannot finish, let me have a bite. Why should this good food go to waste?"

He sat down before the cauldrons, and in a wink he finished all the stew. All you could hear was the bones crackling in his teeth.

They spent the night in the village. It was a fine spot, with lots of shade and cold, pure spring water. Jekovoy decided to take a rest and live there for a while.

"Every day one of us will stay at home and cook our dinner," said Jekovoy, "and the others will go out to hunt."

They drew lots. The first to stay home was Tash Palvan.

When everybody left, Tash Palvan made a fire and sat down to cook a stew in a cauldron with forty handles.

Suddenly a little old man mounted on a goat came to the village. He was no bigger than a man's hand, and his beard was seven elbows long. The goat had a tiny bell tied to each hair on his body, and their jingling spread over all the mountains and valleys.

"Give me some fire," asked the little old man.

"Take it yourself," said Tash Palvan.

The little old man jumped off the goat, ran up to the hearth, picked up the huge cauldron with the forty handles, and in a second he swallowed the boiling stew, spitting out the bones.

"There!" said the little old man. Then he jumped up on his goat and rode off, with a jingling and a tinkling all around.

Tash Palvan turned pale with fright. But there was nothing to be done. He collected the bones, threw them back into the cauldron, filled it with water, and began to cook a soup.

The hunters returned and sat down to their supper. They didn't like the soup. But Jekovoy said nothing. The same thing happened on the second day, and on the third. On the fourth morning Jekovoy said to his giants:

"Today you will go out hunting, and I will stay at home."

As soon as the giants left, Jekovoy made a huge fire and put in it a stone that weighed seven hundred pounds.

Soon the old man on the goat came and asked for some fire.

"Certainly," said Jekovoy, pulled out the red-hot stone

from the fire, and flung it at the old man. The stone struck off the old man's head, and it rolled down the path.

It rolled and winked at Jekovoy:

"Just wait and see! I'll show you! I'll show you!"

Jekovoy ran after the head, but just as he caught up with it, it scuttled down into a burrow and disappeared.

When the giants returned, Jekovoy said:

"We have no more time to go out hunting. Our quarry is right here. Shear off the goat's fur and weave it into a rope, as strong and long as you can make it."

The giants wove and wove, and made a rope one hundred and sixty elbows long.

Jekovoy told the giants to tie one end around Tash Palvan's waist and lower him into the burrow. But when they let him down a little, he started crying:

"Oh, it is dark here! Oh, I am frightened! Pull me out!"

They pulled him out, tied the rope around Kyrs Palvan, and began to let him down. But he also started crying:

"Oh, it's dark here! I'm afraid!"

They let down Cedar Palvan, but he also pleaded:

"Oh, how dark, I am afraid! Pull me up again!"

"Brave heroes!" Jekovoy laughed at the giants. "I guess I'll have to go myself."

He tied the rope around his waist and started down into the burrow.

The giants lowered him a hundred and sixty elbows,

the full length of the rope, but still it did not quite reach the bottom. Jekovoy jumped down, got up on his feet and looked around. He was in a large cave, and before him, in an iron cage, sat a maiden of such beauty as he had never seen before. When she opened her eyes, there was a brightness in the air. When she lowered her lids, twilight fell. When she closed her eyes, dark night came.

Jekovoy stood silent before the beauty, unable to say a word.

And the maiden opened her eyes again, and everything was bright as in the daylight world.

"Why have you come into the Underground Kingdom, young warrior?" she asked him. "If a bird should fly here, it will burn its wings. If a man should come here, he will burn his feet. I pity you."

"I am looking for the head of a wicked little old man with a long beard," said Jekovoy.

"Woe," said the maiden. "It is the head of the most powerful Div Razgun. The head is guarded by seventy thousand djinns. They'll come here and attack you. If you will fight them with your sword, each drop of blood will turn into a new seventy thousand djinns."

"And where can I find these djinns?"

"They're sleeping now. Go and kill them while they sleep. This is the only way to save yourself."

But Jekovoy stood tall and spread his shoulders wide. He proudly raised his head and cried:

"A brave man does not kill a sleeping enemy."

He shouted so loudly that stones began to tumble off the ceiling of the cave, but the djinns only turned from one side to the other. Jekovoy gave a second shout. The mountain shook, the cave walls moved, but the djinns only raised their heads. He gave a third shout—the mountains trembled and their tops began to rock.

The seventy thousand djinns jumped up and looked around.

"Who is that shouting here?" they asked. "Who dares disturb our sleep?"

The head of Div Razgun rolled out of the corner and cried:

"Kill him! Kill him!"

The djinns threw themselves at Jekovoy. He swung his sword and sliced the heads off seven thousand djinns. He swung again, and seven thousand heads rolled off again. But new djinns rose from every drop of blood, and Jekovoy kept fighting them for seven days and seven nights.

When the mighty hero grew tired, the maiden closed her eyes and night came. The djinns, who could not fight in the dark, retreated and Jekovoy rested.

With ever new strength he attacked the hosts of djinns, but finally he began to weaken. And Div Razgun's head kept rolling around and around his feet, shouting:

"I'll show you! I'll show you!"

The maiden closed her eyes again and Jekovoy rested. And when she opened her eyes, he pulled out his hammer and began to hammer the djinns down into the ground. For seven days and seven nights he hammered at them, and drove them all into the ground like so many nails into a log of wood.

With the last blow, Jekovoy drove the head of Div Razgun so deep that it reached the very center of the earth.

The maiden laughed with joy and opened her starry eyes still wider. Everything shone and glimmered in the cave. And the maiden said:

"Now let me out, young hero."

She told him that she had been stolen from her home by Div Razgun, who kept her in a cage because she refused to be his wife. Jekovoy smashed the cage and freed the maiden. She showed him where the div had kept his countless treasures—gold, and silver, and precious stones of every kind.

Jekovoy shouted to the giants:

"Let down the rope!"

He tied a bag of gold to it and told them to pull it up. For fourteen days they pulled and pulled the bags of gold and precious stones out of the cave. At the end, Jekovoy tied the rope around the maiden's waist.

"You must come with me," she said, "or the faithless giants will leave you here."

"No," said Jekovoy. "They've always obeyed me." And he ordered them to pull the maiden out of the Underground Kingdom.

At the very last, he bound the rope around himself and commanded the giants to pull him out. They pulled him up halfway, and then they said:

"No, he defeated us, and he mocked us. Why should we pull him up?"

They cut the rope, and Jekovoy fell down to the bottom of the cave. For seven days he lay there unconscious. When he came to, he started to climb out through the burrow. He climbed, and climbed, until he finally climbed out of the Underground Kingdom.

He looked around—no giants, no maiden, no treasures. Saddened, he turned and went wherever his eyes led him.

Who knows how long he walked, but at long last he came to a stony field which an old man was trying to plow with two oxen.

"Give me some food, father," said Jekovoy. "I have not eaten for many days."

"Do some plowing for me," said the old man, "and I will go home and bring you bread and sheep cheese."

Jekovoy tried to plow, but he found that his strength was gone. He stopped and gave a shout.

In answer to his shout, bears came running from all the mountains. They bowed to him and asked:

"What do you wish, Son of the She-Bear?"

"Plow this field, while I lie down and take a rest."

The bears began to dig the earth with their strong claws. They pulled out the stones and threw them on the side.

The old peasant came back and cried:

"Hey, fellow, send away your bears. I am afraid they'll eat my oxen."

"The bears obey me. They'll do what I tell them. Give me some food."

They ate their lunch, and in the meantime the bears had plowed and cleared the whole field. Jekovoy sent them home and said:

"Whenever this old man calls you, come and help him."

Then Jekovoy, his strength restored, went on and on until he came to a village. He wondered—there was not a single living soul about.

After a long search, he found a man crouching in a pit.

"Why are you hiding in a pit?" he asked the man.

"Forty days ago, the dragon Mundarkho came flying from the mountains. He is an ogre. This is why everyone is hiding."

"And what road leads to the dragon?"

"Go straight up to the mountain. That is where he lives."

"Good," said Jekovoy. "When I shout, you can all come out. It will mean I killed the dragon."

Jekovoy climbed the path to the high mountaintop. On the very summit, above the clouds, lay Mundarkho. He was so huge, he was larger than the mountain.

Jekovoy threw himself upon the dragon with his sword. For three days and three nights he fought him, and in the end he chopped him up to pieces.

Then he walked to the edge of the mountain and gave a mighty shout. The people, rejoicing, came out of their hiding places. They held a great and merry feast, singing the praises of the hero's strength and courage. They begged Jekovoy to stay and live with them.

"I would be glad to, but I cannot," said Jekovoy. "I must find the faithless giants and free the lovely maiden."

And Jekovoy continued on his journey. No one knows how long he walked, but on the way he performed many brave and noble deeds. And at the last he came back to the city of Chimkent. It had been seized by the three giants, Tash Palvan, Kyrs Palvan, and Cedar Palvan.

The giants had levied fifty taxes on the city, till rich and poor alike were left without a bite to eat, while they themselves feasted and drank and made merry day and night. The poor maiden, who refused to feast with them and remained faithful to Jekovoy, had been thrown into a dungeon.

Jekovoy took his bow that weighed seven thousand

pounds and shot a seven-hundred-pound arrow at Tash Palvan. The giant, struck through the heart, swayed and fell dead. Kyrs Palvan jumped up and threw a thousand-pound cudgel at Jekovoy, but Jekovoy merely caught it in midair and threw it back at Kyrs, who toppled, crushed under its weight. Cedar Palvan took fright and ran into the steppe, but he, too, was struck down by Jekovoy's arrow.

Jekovoy broke the dungeon door with one blow of his hammer, and the maiden rushed into his arms. The people of Chimkent, invited to their wedding, feasted forty days and forty nights. Jekovoy distributed among the people half of the wealth he had won from the Div Razgun, and everybody praised his generosity and wished him a long life.

But Jekovoy's adventures were not yet over. There was still one last one that brought peace to his heart. Before the wedding feast was over, messengers came riding from Khan Eron with sad news. The armies of the shah of Kizylbash beleaguered Tashkent, and Eron wrote to his son: "My dear son, help us, come and save the city."

"I would not go to help the khan," said Jekovoy, "but I must help the people."

He stuck his sword into his belt, kissed his bride, and rode off to Tashkent. When he approached the city, he gave a mighty shout. A thousand tigers, a thousand bears, and a thousand wolves came running, and the armies of Kizylbash fled like sand blown away by desert winds.

Khan Eron wept with joy and sorrow. The proud khan begged forgiveness for unknowingly killing the she-bear. He begged forgiveness for suspecting his son and sending him on dangerous errands. He begged Jekovoy to remain in Tashkent and be the heir to the khan's throne.

But Jekovoy said to him: "You are my father, and I am happy to be at peace with you. But I am also the simple son of a kind and simple she-bear. I do not want to be a khan."

He went back to Chimkent and to his star-eyed bride, and lived with her a long and happy life.

And no one dared to raise a hand against the people of Chimkent; no enemies attacked them. For even after Jekovoy became an old man and could no longer lift his hammer and his sword, he merely had to go out on the city wall and give a shout, and all the wild beasts of the world would come to serve the great and just Son of the She-Bear.

THE FOOL

A Turkmenian Tale

n a certain village there lived an old man and his wife. One day the old man was gathering dry twigs for firewood and found a large needle. He put the needle with the twigs, tied the bundle with a rope, and brought it home.

He came home, untied the bundle, and began to look for the needle.

The old woman asked him:

"What are you looking for?"

"A needle."

"Where did you put it?"

"Into this bundle of twigs."

"How silly can you get? If you had stuck the needle into your robe, it would not have been lost!"

"Good," said the old man. "Next time I'll do it."

The next time he went for firewood he found a large wheel axle. We'll make good use of it, he thought, and tried to stick it into his robe. He tore his robe, and finally brought the axle home in his bosom.

"How silly can you get!" cried the old woman. "You should have tied the axle to the rope and dragged it home."

"Good," said the man. "Next time I'll do it."

On the third day he found a little puppy. He tied it to the rope and dragged it home. By the time he brought it home the puppy was almost dead with suffocation. The old woman looked at it and shook her head:

"How silly can you get? You should have called the pup, and it would have followed you!"

"Good," said the old man. "Next time I'll do it."

He went into the steppe, and saw a hare. Remembering his old woman's words, he called the hare and beckoned to it. The hare flicked his little tail and hopped away. The old man came home and said:

"You gave me bad advice, woman. I saw a hare and called him, but he ran away."

"How silly can you get! When you see a hare, you cry, 'Stop like a stone!' The hare will stop and you will catch him."

"Good! Next time I will cry, 'Stop like a stone!' "

The next day the old man met a stranger and shouted:

"Stop like a stone! Stop like a stone!"

The man got angry, thinking the old man was mocking him, and gave him a sound thrashing.

Moaning and groaning, the old man came home and

told his wife what had happened.

"Oh, what can I do with you?" said the old woman. "You should have told the stranger 'A happy day, and many more like it to you!' "

"Good," said the old man. "Now I'll say 'A happy day, and many more like it to you!' "

Two days later the old man met a funeral procession, and shouted to the mourners:

"A happy day, and many more like it to you!"

The people heard this and gave the old man a good beating.

Again he came home groaning, and told his wife about it.

"Oh, what a fool! You should have told them, 'What a misfortune! What a misfortune!' "

"Good! Now I'll say 'What a misfortune!' "

A day later the old man met a merry wedding procession and began to cry:

"Woe is me! What a misfortune! What a misfortune!"

The bridegroom's father heard this, dismounted, and gave the old man another thrashing.

The old man limped home, and said:

"I'll never listen to you again, old woman! Your advice got me all black and blue. From this day on I'll listen to nobody. I'll live by my own brains."

He said that and went into the woods to chop some wood. He climbed up on a thick branch and began to chop it with his axe.

"What are you doing?" cried a passerby. "Why do you chop the branch you're sitting on? You'll fall and hurt yourself!"

And the old man said to him:

"Even if you're telling me the truth, I will not listen to you. I'll live by my own brains."

Soon the branch toppled down, and the old man fell with it and almost broke his back. Groaning, he said:

"The man was right that I would fall. He probably knows everything. Perhaps he knows when I'll die. I'll have to ask him."

The old man caught up with the passerby and asked:

"Tell me, good man, when will I die?"

The passerby laughed aloud and said:

"Your death will come when your donkey stumbles three times on the road."

The old man thanked him kindly and went back to chopping wood.

He loaded the wood on the donkey, and started home.

After a while, the donkey stepped into a hole in the road and stumbled. The old man got frightened.

"Woe is me! One soul has already gone out of me."

The donkey walked some more, and stumbled again. The old man got even more frightened.

"Woe! The second soul is out, too."

A little later the donkey stumbled a third time.

"Well," said the old man. "Now I am altogether dead."

He got down from the donkey, stretched out by the bridge, and lay there for hours without moving an arm or a leg. At first the donkey stood quietly by, waiting. Then he noticed a green clearing, turned off the road, and began to graze.

At that time an apple merchant was driving down the road. His horse shied suddenly and turned over the cart. The merchant tried and tried to straighten up the cart, but could not lift it.

Then he caught sight of the old man by the bridge. He went up to him and asked him:

"Help me to pick up the cart!"

The old man did not move, but merely answered:

"Can't you see? I am a dead man. I cannot help you with anything."

The merchant thought the old man was joking, and he said:

"Stop joking. Get up and help me."

"No," said the old man. "I cannot help you. I'm telling you, I am dead, dead!"

The merchant heard this and he said:

"Just wait a moment, I'll bring you back to life."

And he struck him with his whip.

The old man raised himself a little. The merchant hit him a second time. The old man sat up. The merchant hit him a third time. The old man jumped up on his feet and cried:

"Thank you, my good man, thank you! Because of you I am back among the living."

"Don't thank me. Better help me pick up the cart."

When they straightened out the cart, the old man said:

"Do me a kindness, make me a present of your whip."

The merchant gladly gave it to him.

Beaming with joy, the old man came home, handed the whip to his old woman, and said:

"Hide this whip and guard is well until the day I die. When I am dying, you will bring me back to life with it again."

"What are you talking about?" asked his wife.

And he told her everything that had happened to him that day.

The woman listened to him and shook her head.

"There is a good saying among the people: 'If it were not my fool, I would laugh, too.' Now go to bed and rest your weary bones. You still have many a day left to live by your own foolish brains, whip or no whip. And thank God that you have a kind and patient wife."

THE JACKAL
AND THE POLECAT

A Turkmenian Tale

 polecat met a jackal walking down the road and crying bitterly.

"Why are you crying?" asked the polecat.

"I was told that I will be appointed king of the barnyard."

"Congratulations! You will never go hungry again. What could be better?"

"That's just why I am crying. I am afraid it's too good to be true."

I WAS IN IT

A Turkmenian Tale

ne evening Kemine put on his
sheepskin coat and went to a
neighbor's house, where there was
to be a gathering of friends. At the
doorstep he tripped and fell. He
jumped up at once and, pretending
that nothing had happened, entered the house and
greeted the guests.

"What's wrong with you, Kemine, falling right on
the doorstep?" they asked him.

"I didn't fall," he said. "It was my coat."

"How come it made such a bang?" they asked.

"Oh, that's because I was in it."

FLIES

A Turkmenian Tale

he Sultan Soyun was always carrying on disputes with clever Mirali, intent on winning at least one argument at any cost. One day he said to Mirali:

"These flies will be the death of me. Isn't there a place in the world where there are no flies?"

And Mirali answered: "The only place where there are no flies is where there are no people."

The sultan laughed at Mirali and said:

"Come, get on your horse, let's ride out into the steppe and we shall see."

They mounted their horses and rode off into the wide, deserted steppe.

"Well," said the sultan. "Here there surely are no people. Let's dismount and sit down a while."

In a few minutes there was a loud buzzing, and a fly sat down on the sultan's cheek.

"See, you were wrong, Mirali!" the sultan cried triumphantly. "Isn't that a fly?"

Mirali smiled:

"Aren't we people?"

And so Mirali won the argument again.

TSAP-TSARAP

A Karakalpak Tale

 erhaps it happened, perhaps not, but this is the story they tell. A great rich shah was building a beautiful new city. Men came from all ends of the land to work for the shah. Some dug the earth, some made bricks, others built houses and planted gardens. And everyone who came was paid one tenge a day for his work.

One day Aldar Kose came to the city. He was a poor man, always hungry, nothing but skin and bones, and his robe hung in tatters over his body. The shah looked at his skinny arms, his torn clothes, and said:

"Go away, go away, go back to where you came from. You aren't of any use to me."

But Aldar Kose begged him:

"Your Majesty, give me any work you choose and pay me as little as you wish. If you turn me away, I will die of hunger."

The shah would not listen to him, but Aldar Kose begged and begged, until the shah agreed. He sent him to the most difficult work—mixing clay, and promised to pay him one tenge for a whole year.

Aldar Kose worked diligently and hard all year, and then he went to the treasurer to receive his wage. Everybody else went away with a bag full of coins, but poor Aldar Kose got only a single tenge. He went to the market to see what he could buy for his tenge. He looked at the silk and velvet clothes, at the fine brass and silver and rugs, at the fruit and the fish. But what can you buy for a single tenge? He walked and walked until he got tired. So he sat down on the bank of the stream that wound its way through the city, and looked sadly at the water. Suddenly he saw an old woman walking past. She carried a bag, with something jumping, growling, and hissing in it.

"What do you have there?" Aldar Kose asked her.

"My Tsap-Tsarap," said the old woman. "My Catch-and-Scratch. I want to sell him."

"And what's the good of your Tsap-Tsarap?" asked Aldar Kose.

"Oh, my Tsap-Tsarap is a great guardian of grain and rice, a mighty killer of rats and mice," said the old woman.

"And how much do you want for your Tsap-Tsarap?"

"If you give me a tenge, I'll let you have him."

Aldar Kose gave her his tenge, slung the sack with

Tsap-Tsarap over his shoulder, and walked away. He walked and walked until he came to a barn full of newly harvested corn, and near the barn he saw a man with a wooden stick.

"Why do you sit here?" asked Aldar Kose. "What are you guarding, and from whom?"

And the man with the stick answered:

"Oh, don't even ask—I am in trouble. I have just harvested the corn, and now I must thresh it, but I cannot take a step away from the barn. There's an army of mice around, and they'll eat up all the grain. I have no remedy against the mice."

"Oh, I have a good remedy against them," said Aldar Kose.

"What is is?"

"It's right here in my bag; its name is Tsap-Tsarap."

And the owner of the corn began to plead with Aldar Kose:

"Lend me your Tsap-Tsarap, I'll pay you anything you ask."

They agreed on twenty tenge, and Aldar Kose let Tsap-Tsarap out of the bag. He was a huge, healthy tom. He didn't even play with the mice, just caught them and killed them one by one. In two hours he killed a thousand mice, and the owner of the barn was so happy he said to Aldar Kose:

"Oh, what a great beast that is! More terrible than a tiger. Sell him to me, and I'll be able to sleep nights again."

But Aldar Kose wouldn't think of it. He put Tsap-Tsarap back into his bag and went on.

He walked and walked, until he came back to the beautiful rich city that he had helped build for the shah.

He passed the shah's great treasury and saw all the soldiers running and swinging sticks and shouting "Kish-kish." The shah's musicians stood around beating drums, blowing into their pipes, and everything was in an up-roar.

"What happened?" asked Aldar Kose. "Why are you running around like madmen, swinging sticks and shouting 'Kish-kish!' and beating your drums and blowing into your pipes? Has the shah's treasury been attacked by a thousand robbers?"

And the soldiers shouted at him:

"Get away from here, tramp. Don't bother us! It's worse than a thousand robbers. Nothing helps—neither 'Kish-kish!' nor drums, nor sticks, nor pipes. Woe, woe! We're lost!"

"Stop running around and tell me what happened," said Aldar Kose. "What is the trouble? Perhaps I can help you."

"Our trouble is a horde of mice. They're not afraid of anything. They've chewed up the shah's gold-embroidered robes and his precious silks, and now they're getting at the money. Our shah declared: 'If you don't find a remedy against the mice, I'll chop your heads off!' And so we are running all around, trying to scare off the mice, but nothing helps."

"You silly people," said Aldar Kose. "I have an excellent remedy against the mice."

"What remedy?"

"The name of it is Tsap-Tsarap."

The soldiers called the shah's chief vizier, and he said to Aldar Kose:

"Lend us your Tsap-Tsarap. I'll pay you two hundred tenge."

Aldar Kose let Tsap-Tsarap out of the bag, and he began to run after the mice and kill them one by one. Those he did not kill ran off and away as fast as they could.

"Oh, what a fine beast!" cried the vizier. "Sell him to us! Then our heads will be safe, and the shah's treasures will be safe."

"He's not for sale," said Aldar Kose.

The vizier begged and begged:

"I'll give you a thousand tenge. Sell us Tsap-Tsarap! We'll surely lose our heads without him."

"He's not for sale," insisted Aldar Kose.

The vizier began to cry:

"Sell us Tsap-Tsarap! We'll give you six camels loaded with bags of gold."

And Aldar Kose took the six camels and the gold, bought himself a house and garden, and began to live without worrying where his next meal was coming from.

The vizier put Tsap-Tsarap into the shah's treasure house. In a week he caught all the mice and there was nothing more for him to do. He got very bored, and went out for a walk. He wandered around the rooms and the courtyards of the shah's palace, and finally came to the richest room, where the shah sat on his fine carved throne. "That's a good place to sharpen my claws," thought Tsap-Tsarap, and he began to scratch his claws on the leg of the throne, purring with pleasure.

When the shah saw the strange beast clawing at his throne, he got so frightened that he began to shout:

"Hey, viziers! Hey, guardsmen! What is this terrible wild beast?"

The chief vizier came running and reported:

"It's Tsap-Tsarap, Your Majesty."

"What sort of Tsap-Tsarap is this? What does he do?"

"He catches and kills all . . ."

"Help!" cried the shah before the vizier had time to finish, jumped off his throne, and rushed away.

The shah ran, and Tsap-Tsarap ran after him. The shah ran into the next room, and Tsap-Tsarap ran after him. The shah ran into a third room, and Tsap-Tsarap ran after him. They ran and ran, until the shah came to the royal stable, jumped up on a horse, and galloped away. And of course, Tsap-Tsarap could not keep up with him.

So he walked around some more through the palace and the grounds, then he went out to see the city, then he found the house of Aldar Kose and settled there. Aldar Kose fed him well. Tsap-Tsarap rubbed his head against Aldar Kose's leg, sat in his lap, and purred with pleasure. At night he hunted mice. In the morning he slept, warming himself in sunny spots.

When the shah found out about it, he flew into a rage and ordered his viziers:

"I know this Aldar Kose—he's always full of tricks. It's all his fault. Take your bows and arrows, mount your horses, and go at once to the house of Aldar Kose. Shoot Tsap-Tsarap, and bring me his skin and his master's head. I'll teach Aldar Kose how to make fun of his shah."

The viziers jumped on their fast horses, prepared their bows and arrows, and galloped off.

And Aldar Kose knew nothing at all about it. He was busy in his garden, and Tsap-Tsarap lay stretched out on the fence, purring in the sun.

The viziers rode up to Aldar Kose's house and wanted to come into the yard. At this moment Tsap-Tsarap stood up, arched his back, stretched his front paws, then his hind ones, and jumped off the fence. And landed right on the back of the chief vizier's horse. The chief vizier looked over his shoulder and saw Tsap-Tsarap behind him, his yellow eyes blazing in the sun.

"Help!" cried the chief vizier. "He wants to kill me!" And he tumbled off his horse, jumped up, and rushed out of the yard. When the other viziers saw Tsap-Tsarap, they also tumbled off their horses and ran after the chief vizier.

The frightened horses galloped back to the palace.

The shah sat at his window waiting for his viziers to bring Tsap-Tsarap's skin and Aldar Kose's head. Suddenly he saw the first horse galloping madly, raising clouds of dust, with Tsap-Tsarap in the saddle, eyes blazing, fur bristling on his back, tail raised, mouth snarling, and claws tearing at the saddle.

"He's killed all my viziers, and now he's coming after me! Help, help!" cried the shah, and fell down dead with fright.

And all the courtiers and all the guards scattered in panic, leaving the palace and the town where such a frightful beast was about.

Tsap-Tsarap jumped off the horse and took a walk through the palace and the grounds. No people. No mice. After a while he got bored again and went back home, to Aldar Kose, where they live peacefully to this day.

A HUNDRED LIES

A Karakalpak Tale

ong ago there lived a khan who was tyrannical and cranky and full of silly, cruel whims. The only good thing about him was that he had a beautiful daughter. An endless line of suitors came to ask for her in marriage: high-born warriors, and beks, and beys, and even khans and shahs.

But the khan declared for all the world to hear that he would give his daughter only to the man who could tell him a hundred lies in succession. And if a suitor failed, his head would be chopped off.

Despite this, suitors came and came, but no one could invent a hundred lies. No matter how they tried, some truth would slip in, and heads fell right and left, regardless of wealth or rank, until there was a mountain of heads in the khan's yard. His daughter wept and pleaded with her father, but there was nothing she could do to sway him.

151

One day a poor, unknown shepherd came to the khan and said:

"I am not a famous warrior, or a bek, or a bey, or a khan, or a shah. I am not even a rich merchant. But I will lie to you a hundred times, and I will not only marry your daughter, but I will also take away your throne."

"You impudent liar!" cried the khan. "Who has ever heard of a ragged shepherd marrying a khan's daughter and taking his throne from him?"

"There, you see, I've told my first lie."

"Go on," commanded the khan.

The shepherd began:

"Before I was born, I herded my great-grandfather's sheep. I was the best shepherd in the land. My father was so pleased with me that when our gray mare gave birth to a foal my father saddled it for me before it could stand up and suckle its mother. Within an hour, the foal grew into a large, spotted mare, and I rode her in the sky and all the way up to the stars. Two days later she disappeared. I looked and looked for her, but could not find her anywhere. I climbed the highest mountain, but I could not see her. I went down into the valleys, but I could not see her. Then I stuck my shepherd's staff into the back of the mare who wasn't there, and started climbing up and up, but still I could not see her. The staff was made of nut wood, and suddenly it started sprouting leaves and branches. The higher I climbed, the taller it grew. It blossomed and bore fruit. I climbed and ate all the nuts I could pick. By that time, I looked around and could see nothing but thick clouds. I swept the clouds away with my whip and closed my eyes tight. And then I saw: beyond six seas and seven mountains, just this side of them, my mare stood looking at the moon. Then she neighed loudly, and gave birth to a foal. Right after that she went on grazing in the lush green meadow under the bright sun, and the newborn foal kept leaping back and forth over her.

"I made a boat from the sheath of my knife, used the blade as an oar, and set out at once to get my mare. But the moment I sailed, I sank to the bottom. I didn't lose my head, but made a boat out of the knife blade and an oar of the sheath, paddled up to the surface, and went on. Before I counted five, I was there. I mounted my mare, and slung the foal across her back before me, and turned homeward. But as soon as we began to swim, we started drowning again. Without thinking long, I mounted the foal, and threw the mare across his back before me. In the twinkling of an eye, we were across the river."

"River!" said the khan. "It must have been an irrigation ditch."

"Maybe so," said the shepherd, "but it took a bird from dawn to dusk to fly across it, and in the end the poor bird was so tired that it could barely move its wings."

"It must have been a tiny fledgling," said the khan.

"Maybe so, but when I caught it I could not bring it into my tent; its tail and half its body remained outside."

"You must have had a tent big enough for a mouse."

"Maybe so," said the shepherd. "But when a donkey brayed at the door, you could not hear it at the other end."

"It must have been a beetle, not a donkey."

"Maybe so," answered the shepherd. "But when we went out hunting, sixty hunters rode on the donkey's back. And he was so fast that each of us caught a hare without getting off."

"Oh, to the devil with your donkey," cried the khan. "Go on with your story."

And the shepherd continued:

"When the foal was swimming across the river, with the mare on his back in front of me, I saw a rabbit running on the water. I took a needle from the collar of my robe, threw it at the rabbit and killed it. Then I felt like eating some nice roast rabbit and decided to make a fire. I gathered twigs and piled them up, but they crawled off in all directions; it turned out that they were snakes. Then I gathered more twigs and made a fire. When I opened the rabbit, there were sixty pounds of fat in it. I cut up the rabbit and wanted to put one leg aside for later, but I could not lift it. So I put all the meat, together with the leg, into a bottomless kettle and put it on the fire. There was a huge pile of roast meat. My mouth begged: 'Give me a piece!' But my hand answered: 'I will not.' My teeth, I remember, chewed something, but nothing came into my stomach.

"After that I took the sixty pounds of fat and started greasing my boots. But there was only enough for one. By that time I was so tired that I stretched out on the ground to rest, putting my boots under my head so that no one would steal them. I fell asleep at once, but was awakened by wild shouting. I raised my head and saw my boots fighting. The one that had not been greased yelled: 'You were greased, and I was left dry.' I sat up, slapped them both on the cheeks, and went back to sleep. In the morning the ungreased boot was gone. I put on the greased boot on both my feet and ran to catch up with the other. I ran for seven days and seven nights but never caught up with it. On the way I passed three wells. Two were dry, and in the third there wasn't a single drop of water. In each well a fish was swimming. One wasn't alive, and the other two were dead. I found three pots. Two were broken, the third had no bottom. I cleaned the fattest fish and cooked myself a soup in the broken pots, without water, and without salt, and without fire. The soup was saltier than brine—the best soup I have ever eaten.

"After I had my fill, I went on again to look for my ungreased boot; without leaving the spot, I ran as fast as a camel for another seven days and seven nights. Then suddenly I lost its track. I couldn't imagine where it could have disappeared. I looked around and saw a village, so I walked in and found that it was inhabited by little bugs, not people. Their village elder had died that day, and they were holding a funeral feast. I took another look—and there was my ungreased boot serving the guests, carrying bowls with food here and there. I glowered at it, but it immediately brought me a plate of meat. I ate the meat, caught the boot, put it on, and continued on my way. Before I walked ten steps, I was hungry again. Then I was tormented by thirst. My throat was so dry I could not swallow. And before me lay an endless desert, with the sun baking mercilessly. Suddenly I noticed a lake right in the middle of the burning desert. I ran up to it, but it was frozen. I tried to break the ice with my boots, with an axe, with a crowbar, but it was so thick that it wouldn't break. Then I carefully took my head off my shoulders and banged it on the ice. It made a hole large enough to water forty horses. I pulled all the water from the lake into my mouth and felt something cool and tasty on my tongue. It turned out that, together with the water, I had pulled in all the fish that lived in the lake. I let the water pour out and ate the fish. Having eaten and drunk, I felt strong again and walked homeward with a brisk, rapid stride. Then I met some men from my village, and they started laughing and could not stop.

" 'What's wrong' I asked them, but they kept laughing so hard they could not speak. At last one of them said: 'Hey, where is your head?' I felt for it—it wasn't there.

Then I remembered I had left it by the lake. I ran back to the lake. By that time, sixty ducks and sixty geese had built nests in my head, laid their eggs, and were sitting on them, waiting for the goslings and duck-lings to hatch. I chased off the birds, put my head back in place, and wanted to go home, when sixty ants caught at the bottom of my robe and would not let me go. They wanted me to be their guest at dinner.

"I went with them to the ant village. They sat me down in the place of honor, in nine rooms at once. The master of the house said: 'For such a fine guest, put a camel's thigh into the kettle.' When they served it, I saw that it was not a camel's thigh, but a grasshopper's. I took a knife and sliced it until there was a mountain of meat. I ate until I was full and then divided the rest among the master's wives and children. Then I said good-bye and left.

"Suddenly I heard a loud quarreling. To hear it better, I stuffed my ears, and discovered that the quarrel was between my knife and its sheath. The sheath was saying: 'You have an easy life. You gorge yourself on meat, then you stick your nose into me and go to sleep. And I don't get even a crumb to eat.' And the knife answered: 'But when I stick my nose into you, you strangle me until I cannot breathe.' I smiled, but said nothing and went on. It took me five days to reach the place where I had tied my mare. When I came there, I found that she had foaled ten times again, and now I was the owner of a fine herd of horses. But as soon as I untied the mare, they all scattered and ran away, and now I am about to send my boots to look for them."

The shepherd was silent a while, then he said to the khan:

"Great khan, I lied to you a hundred times, and now you must give me your daughter."

The Khan had long lost count of the lies, but he immediately cried:

"You're lying, miserable wretch! You've told me only ninety-nine lies, not a hundred. Hey, executioner, off with his head!"

But the shepherd was not frightened. He bowed and smiled:

"Honorable khan, you have counted correctly. I told you only ninety-nine lies. But when I said 'a hundred,' it was another lie, and that makes it exactly a hundred."

The khan had no choice but to let his daughter marry the shepherd. He was so good at telling tales that she was never bored with him. They lived very happily together, but after a while they got tired of the khan's silly whims. The shepherd drove him out and took the throne. And all the people rejoiced, because he was a wise and clever khan.

DATE DUE

Jan 24 '74			
Oct 10 '74			
Feb 22 '77			
Jan 10 '78			
Mar 14 '79			
Oct 8 '81			

Metropolitan School District
of
Washington Township
Indianapolis, Indiana 46240